La Maison Suspendue

La Maison Suspendue

by Michel Tremblay
translated by John Van Burek

Talonbooks • Vancouver • 1991

copyright © 1990 Leméac Editeur
translation copyright © 1991 John Van Burek

published with assistance from the Canada Council

Talonbooks
201 / 1019 East Cordova Street
Vancouver, British Columbia
Canada V6A 1M8

This book was typeset in Century Oldstyle by Pièce de Résistance Ltée., and printed and bound in Canada by Hignell Printing Ltd.

First printing: September 1991

Rights to produce *La Maison Suspendue*, in whole or in part, in any medium by any group, amateur or professional, are retained by the author. Interested persons are requested to apply to his agent, John C. Goodwin et Associés, 839 Sherbrooke est, Suite 2, Montréal, Québec H2L 1K6.

Canadian Cataloguing in Publication Data

Tremblay, Michel, 1942–
    [Maison suspendue. English]
    La maison suspendue

    A play.
    Translation of: La Maison suspendue.
    ISBN 0-88922-295-9

    I. Title   II. Title: Maison suspendue. English.
PS8539.R47M313 1991   C842'.54   C91-091643-8
PQ3919.2.T73M313 1991

CHARACTERS

1910:
VICTOIRE, in her thirties
JOSAPHAT-LE-VIOLON
  in his thirties
GABRIEL, 11

1950:
LA GROSSE FEMME, 48
ALBERTINE, 41
ÉDOUARD, 40
MARCEL, 11

1990:
JEAN-MARC, 48
MATHIEU, 30
SÉBASTIEN, 11

La Maison Suspendue was first performed by Compagnie Jean Duceppe at the Place des Arts in Montréal, Québec, on September 12, 1990, with the following cast:

Josaphat	Jean-Marc	Élise Guilbault
La Grosse Femme	Gabriel	Rita Lafontaine
Victoire	Marcel	Jean-Louis Millette
Albertine	Sébastien	Michel Poirer
Édouard	Yves Desgagnés	Gilles Renaud
Mathieu	Denise Gagnon	

Hugolin Chevrette-Landesque

Directed by André Brassard.

With set design by Michel Crête, costumes by François Barbeau, lighting by Luc Prairie, and original music by André Gagnon.

La Maison Suspendue was first performed in English by The Canadian Stage Company in Toronto, Ontario on November 30, 1990, with the following cast:

Josaphat	Jean-Marc	Léa-Marie Cantin
La Grosse Femme	Gabriel	Diana Leblanc
Victoire	Marcel	Claude Gai
Albertine	Sébastien	Simon Fortin
Édouard	Pierre Powers	Guy Thauvette
Mathieu	Charlotte Boisjoli	

Gideon Arthurs/Jean-François Bard

Directed by John Van Burek.

With set design by Michael Eagan, costumes by Charlotte Dean, lighting by Steven Hawkins, English dialogue coaching by Lin Joyce, and original violin music by Taras Chornowol.

La Maison Suspendue

The set represents the log cabin house at Duhamel, the beginning of a beautiful evening in July.

A strange and powerful energy emanates from this house, as if the history of the entire world had taken place here.

JEAN-MARC and Mathieu enter, carrying luggage.

JEAN-MARC:
> Nothing's changed. Well, almost nothing. Just the hydro lines and the TV antenna that I saw in the back . . . Incredible, isn't it? When I came to see it in the spring, I was afraid I'd find it completely transformed. You know what they do to old houses, nowadays . . . but when I came up the path from the road, I had the impression I was returning to my childhood. Everything was the same . . . the colours, the sounds, the smells . . . Obviously the trees are bigger, but they're the same trees . . .

MATHIEU:
> Is that why you bought it? To re-live your childhood?

JEAN-MARC: *(smiling)*
> Could be . . .

MATHIEU:
> It's rustic, that's for sure!

JEAN-MARC:
> I told you, Mathieu, it's a log cabin that hasn't changed in a hundred years . . .

MATHIEU:
> I'm not criticizing, simply stating the facts . . .

JEAN-MARC:
> You didn't have to come . . .

MATHIEU:
> Listen, we'll be fine here. Sébastien and I will get used to it . . . We're only here for two weeks . . . After that, we'll leave you to work in peace . . . Aie, my first house in the country. I've almost got the jitters. Me, I'm a city boy, I don't know country life . . . I mean, not the real country . . . Like this.

JEAN-MARC:
> Me neither, for that matter . . . I've always been happy to use my friends' places in the country . . . Even this, you can tell, I haven't been here very often . . .

MATHIEU:
> In any case, it's beautiful . . . It's impressive, all this, the lake, the mountains . . . It might even be a bit oppressive, but it's impressive . . .

> *He takes a deep breath.*

Even the smell is amazing. There's, like a bite in the air.
I have the feeling if I breathe too deeply, I'll get drunk!
That'd be nice, hein? Roll around on the ground because
the air you breathe is too pure! It'd be different, that's
for sure . . . The smell of the pines, does it stick
around or does it disappear after a few hours, like the
smell of the sea? *(He is clearly not at ease. He heaves a
big sigh.)*

JEAN-MARC:
You'd give anything to be somewhere else, wouldn't
you?

MATHIEU:
Right this minute, yes . . . I'd get in the car and I'd go
back to Montréal, with the noise and the heat . . . But
I'll be okay . . . After the first night, I'll be okay . . . I
hope. I can't stand it when I'm like this . . . I mean, I
have every reason in the world to be happy here . . .

SÉBASTIEN comes in carrying a small suitcase.

SÉBASTIEN:
Jean-Marc, did you check to see if the TV works?

MATHIEU:
Sébastien, we just got here!

JEAN-MARC:
We're not even in the house, yet . . .

SÉBASTIEN:
Yeah, but it's important!

MATHIEU:
Don't worry, it's going to work, your Nintendo.

9

JEAN-MARC:
The colours may not be to your liking, but I'm pretty sure it'll work. There's an antenna on the roof.

SÉBASTIEN:
Le Nintendo doesn't need an antenna!

MATHIEU and JEAN-MARC look at one another.

MATHIEU:
What do you mean, it doesn't need an antenna?

SÉBASTIEN:
Ben, in the city, if you unplug the cable, the picture's lousy, but if you plug in le Nintendo, it works fine!

JEAN-MARC and MATHIEU:
Really?

SÉBASTIEN looks at the house for the first time.

SÉBASTIEN:
Is this the house?

JEAN-MARC:
This is it . . .

SÉBASTIEN:
And we're gonna stay here for two weeks?

MATHIEU:
That's right, and we're gonna love it, Sébastien!

SÉBASTIEN:
Well, we'll try, hein? Are there ghosts at least?

JEAN-MARC:
You bet! At least three! One for each bedroom. One of them limps, one's blind in one eye, and the other one has no head . . .

SÉBASTIEN:
I'll take the room with the one with no head . . .

SÉBASTIEN has come closer to the house.

SÉBASTIEN:
Did you use to live here, Jean-Marc?

JEAN-MARC:
No, no . . . But I used to visit, when I was your age . . .

SÉBASTIEN:
Is it true there are snakes?

JEAN-MARC:
Well, there used to be . . . "in my time", as you always put it . . .

SÉBASTIEN:
Yech . . .

He takes refuge on the first step of the porch. We immediately hear the strain of a fiddle.

SÉBASTIEN:
Do they come into the house?

JEAN-MARC:
They don't know it's a house, Sébastien, they just go wherever they like . . .

SÉBASTIEN:
Do they climb in the beds?

JEAN-MARC:
You want me to scare you, is that it? First it was ghosts, now it's snakes . . .

MATHIEU:
Sébastien, Jean-Marc doesn't have time for scary stories, we have to get settled in . . . *(With a smile)* It's scary enough as it is . . . How long is it since anyone's lived here?

JEAN-MARC looks for his keys.

JEAN-MARC:
Ahh . . . the bloody key . . . It hasn't been that long . . . I'm sure it's liveable . . .

MATHIEU: *(looking towards the lake)*
Wow, at this time of day, you can almost look straight at the sun without hurting your eyes. I bet the sunsets here are fabulous, eh?

JEAN-MARC: *(having found his key)*
Yep. We bring the chairs out onto the porch . . . It's the most beautiful show on earth . . . Okay, in we go . . .

SÉBASTIEN:
How come the porch goes all the way round the house, Jean-Marc?

JEAN-MARC:
Because it's beautiful all the way round the house, Sébastien.

All three of them are up on the verandah. The sound of the fiddle grows louder.

They go inside.

As soon as they close the door behind them, it suddenly opens again and VICTOIRE, dressed as in 1910, comes out of the house.

VICTOIRE:
Josaphat!

She waits a few seconds, then goes toward the right hand end of the verandah.

Josaphat, it's beautiful, what you're playing!

JOSAPHAT: *(off)*
It's nice, hein?

VICTOIRE:
It's new?

The fiddle stops after a few bars.

JOSAPHAT-LE-VIOLON enters, brandishing his fiddle and bow.

JOSAPHAT:
You bet it's new, it's not even finished!

VICTOIRE:
Well, don't stop. Why did you stop?

JOSAPHAT:
I'm going back. I'm just happy to hear you like it . . .

13

He turns and starts back.

VICTOIRE:
You're playing early, tonight . . .

JOSAPHAT:
Eh, oui . . .

VICTOIRE:
You sure it's not too early?

JOSAPHAT has disappeared into the woods.

JOSAPHAT: *(off)*
Look to the south, Victoire, you'll see.

She looks toward the south.

VICTOIRE:
Ha! Sure enough! Look at that! She's come up! Maudit charmer!

JOSAPHAT: *(off)*
What'd you say?

VICTOIRE:
I said you'll never change!

JOSAPHAT: *(off)*
Why should I? I'm perfect the way I am!

The sound of the fiddle rises again.

VICTOIRE: *(to herself)*
I'm gonna end up believing it's true, big brother, that it's you who makes the moon come up every night! He must spend half his time, his nose buried in the almanac!

The door to the house bursts open. SÉBASTIEN runs out.

SÉBASTIEN:
I left it in the car!

MATHIEU comes out after him.

MATHIEU: *(smiling)*
You ninny! The whole way up here, all you talked about was your bloody Nintendo, and you don't even remember to take it out of the car!

MATHIEU catches his son by the collar.

MATHIEU:
Aie, is it okay, Sébastien? I mean, the house?

SÉBASTIEN:
It's not that cool, but it's got a nice smell . . .

SÉBASTIEN goes out stage right.

MATHIEU watches the sunset.

VICTOIRE:
The black flies are finished. We can sit out on the verandah. Josaphat's pipe will chase away the mosquitoes. *(She looks at the sun. She smiles.)* That's right, time for bed, you old bugger. You've done your work for today. Like the rest of us. *(She looks in the direction of Josaphat.)* Well, like me, anyway. *(She sits on the first step of the verandah.)*
It's nice when the boards are still warm, like this. You don't need a chair, and it's as if the wood was softer. And it's not too hot, like it is at noon, it's just warm. That means the day is finally over. I wish it could

15

always be just half an hour before sundown. I bet the world would be a better place.

JEAN-MARC has come out and stands behind MATHIEU.

JEAN-MARC:
What are you doing?

MATHIEU:
Before I met you, I never looked at the sky. It's funny, hein? It's you who taught me that. In any case, out here, I'll get my fill, 'cause it's huge!

JEAN-MARC:
Is it gonna be all right? The house?

MATHIEU:
It's not that cool. But it's got a nice smell.

After a few seconds, the fiddle stops.

JEAN-MARC and MATHIEU turn to go back into the house. JEAN-MARC holds back and doesn't go in right away.

LA GROSSE FEMME, ALBERTINE and ÉDOUARD come in, sinking under the weight of their luggage. They are dressed "very 1950's".

ÉDOUARD:
Another half hour, and my ass was right out of commission.

ALBERTINE:
Édouard, franchement! You promised, no smutty cracks for the whole week! You behaved yourself in the car, ben continue . . .

LA GROSSE FEMME:
Bartine, franchement! It's a joke!

ALBERTINE: *(indicating her brother)*
That's right, be on his side! This'll be one hell of a week!

ÉDOUARD:
Didn't we tell you, the only reason we brought you here was to get you enraged? We decided to have you blow up once and for all before the end of the week . . . I bet you'd be a goner by Wednesday, but our sister-in-law, she's so generous, she thinks you'll hold out til Friday . . .

LA GROSSE FEMME: *(playing along)*
Édouard . . . we said we wouldn't start til tomorrow . . .

ÉDOUARD:
I can't help myself, I'm just itching to begin!

ALBERTINE:
Keep it up and I'll explode right now, then we'll spend the week like cats and dogs . . .

ÉDOUARD:
Tiens, speaking of cats . . .

MATHIEU and SÉBASTIEN return.

SÉBASTIEN, however, without having undergone any physical change, has become MARCEL. He will also become GABRIEL later on. MATHIEU is carrying the Nintendo. MARCEL is holding up an empty bird cage. After a lovely riff, the fiddle stops.

17

MATHIEU: *(half jokingly)*
I'd rather carry it myself, you might trip on a
rock . . . Why don't you watch the sunset while I plug
in the monster. At least you'll get a glimpse of the
country before you glue your nose to the TV for the
next two weeks . . .

SÉBASTIEN:
I brought my bathing suit, you know, and I plan to use it . . .

MATHIEU goes into the house.

ALBERTINE:
Me, when I see him coming with his empty bird cage . . .

MARCEL:
It's for Duplessis . . .

ALBERTINE:
I know it's for Duplessis, that's what drives me crazy!

MARCEL:
I was afraid he'd be sick and I didn't want him to make
a mess . . . And we couldn't find a cat cage, so I took
grand-moman Victoire's old bird cage . . . Duplessis
doesn't mind . . . *(Looking in the cage)* Hein,
Duplessis?

ALBERTINE sighs in desperation.

LA GROSSE FEMME:
Marcel, we agreed to let you bring Duplessis on
condition you wouldn't talk about him and you wouldn't
talk to him. At least, not in front of your mother.

MARCEL:
I didn't talk about him, she did!

18

ALBERTINE:
I didn't talk about your cat!

MARCEL:
No, but you talked about his cage!

ALBERTINE:
Bon, ben, c'est ça, it's my fault again . . .

ÉDOUARD tries to take the bird cage.

MARCEL:
Non, non, I'll keep it with me . . .

ALBERTINE:
Marcel, you're not going to spend the week with that cage in your hand.

ÉDOUARD: *(to Marcel)*
We have to take the luggage inside, Marcel. I'll set it on the kitchen table . . .

MARCEL:
Non, I don't want you to touch it.

ÉDOUARD:
Why not?

MARCEL: *(glancing in his mother's direction)*
I just don't, that's all . . .

ÉDOUARD:
So, your mother's warned you against me? You want my advice, kid, if I were you, I'd watch out for her . . .

ALBERTINE:
Édouard!

ÉDOUARD has knelt down next to MARCEL.

ÉDOUARD:
Your cat doesn't bother me, Marcel . . . You can tell
me about him as much as you like . . . If you want,
we'll go for walks, all three of us . . . Just let her try
and stop us, hein?

MARCEL:
Can you see Duplessis?

ÉDOUARD:
Non. I can't see him. But if it'll make you happy, I can
pretend to see him . . .

MARCEL:
Okay . . .

He lets ÉDOUARD take the cage.

ÉDOUARD goes up the steps of the verandah.

ÉDOUARD:
S'il vous plaît, mesdames, the drama will continue
inside . . . We have to get settled before nightfall,
otherwise poor Albertine will have nasty
nightmares . . . She's so delicate!

*ALBERTINE, LA GROSSE FEMME and
ÉDOUARD go into the house. MARCEL has come to
sit down beside VICTOIRE.*

VICTOIRE:
Gabriel, where have you come from, looking like that?
You been playing by the crique again?

GABRIEL:
  I saw a garter snake. But it was too far out in the water, I couldn't catch it.

VICTOIRE: *(showing him the sunset)*
  Look, isn't it beautiful . . .

GABRIEL:
  You and mon oncle Josaphat, you always want me to watch the sunset . . . It's always the same!

VICTOIRE:
  It's never the same, Gabriel! You must learn to look at these things! *(walking away from him, to herself)* You sure aren't like your father! Him with his head in the clouds and you so down to earth, always got your hands in the dirt, or the water of Lac Simon.

  Meanwhile, JOSAPHAT has returned.

  Eh ben, speak of the devil . . .

JOSAPHAT:
  Speaking of the devil, Gabriel, did you see him go by? I saw him sneaking around about half an hour ago . . .

GABRIEL:
  Hein!

VICTOIRE:
  Josaphat, s'il vous plaît . . .

JOSAPHAT: *(miming as he tells)*
  I don't know if somebody hurt him or what, but he was limping, and he dragged his foot . . . Like this: "Wait for me! Aie, wait for me . . . !"

GABRIEL laughs.

You wouldn't laugh if you'd seen him, mon p'tit gars . . . Moé, he's afraid of me, so when he saw me, he kept right on going, but if it had been you . . . *(He approaches Gabriel, limping.)*

GABRIEL: *(who knows what's coming)*
Non, non, mon oncle Josaphat, not that, not that . . .

To the child's delight, JOSAPHAT throws himself on him and starts to tickle him. A full blown tickling session takes place on the verandah, despite vehement protests from VICTOIRE.

VICTOIRE:
Josaphat, s'il vous plaît . . . stop it . . . You'll get him all wound up, he'll be in an awful state . . . He won't sleep . . . Josaphat! I'm talking to you!

The session ends with the two partners exhausted.

JOSAPHAT:
Ouf . . . J'ai chaud . . .

GABRIEL:
Moé-si . . .

VICTOIRE:
I'm going into the house to get you each a cup of water . . . but don't drink it too fast . . .

While she has been speaking, JEAN-MARC and MATHIEU have come out on the verandah with old, wicker chairs.

JEAN-MARC:
>   I'd never have thought these chairs still existed. This
>   was my favourite . . . It was too big for me and I felt
>   like a king when I sat in it . . . My feet didn't reach
>   the ground and the arms were too high . . .

>   *He sits down.*

MATHIEU:
>   You really sure it's the same one?

JEAN-MARC: *(smiling)*
>   Let me think it is . . .

MATHIEU:
>   Let's just hope we can sit outside, that it's not the
>   International Festival of Black Flies . . .

JEAN-MARC:
>   Non, non, the black flies are finished. In July, it's the
>   mosquitoes.

MATHIEU:
>   Mosquitoes who weigh two and a half pounds and walk
>   off with a whole steak?

JEAN-MARC:
>   You've got it. But there's a breeze tonight, they
>   shouldn't be too bad.

MATHIEU:
>   I brought the Muskoil. Not exactly romantic, eh? Stink
>   to high heaven in such beautiful surroundings . . .

JOSAPHAT:
>   Gabriel, how would you like to go and live in the city?

GABRIEL:
In the city? In St-Jérôme?

JOSAPHAT:
Non, non, in the real city. In Morial.

GABRIEL:
There're too many people in Morial.

JOSAPHAT:
How do you know that, hein, that there're so many people in Morial? Your mother's already talked to you, has she? And she told you to play dumb . . .

GABRIEL looks in the direction of the sunset.

GABRIEL:
Look, isn't it beautiful . . .

JOSAPHAT laughs.

JOSAPHAT:
You're not too good an actor, Gabriel. If ever we move to Morial, we won't take you along to "les soirées de famille", that's for sure!

VICTOIRE comes out of the house with two glasses of water. We hear a scream from inside the house.

ALBERTINE: *(off)*
A spider! There's a spider in my room!

ÉDOUARD: *(off)*
You can have my room, Bartine, I've only got mice!

VICTOIRE:
Don't drink too fast, cold water gives you the runs.

JOSAPHAT and GABRIEL make a face and mutter the same words. He and GABRIEL laugh. VICTOIRE smiles.

JEAN-MARC:
My father told me it was right here in front of the house that his oncle Josaphat made up his most wonderful stories . . . That is, his uncle, in a manner of speaking . . .

The light has dwindled during the last few minutes.

MATHIEU:
It's kind of scary when the sun disappears behind the mountain, don't you think? I mean, surrounded by mountains like this . . . it's like . . . it's like we're in a hole . . .

JEAN-MARC:
In fact we are . . . Lac Simon was the crater of a volcano . . . And just over there to the right, there's a stream that flows down to the lake . . . my grandmother called it a crique, probably because of the word "creek" . . . Come and see . . .

They get up and, stepping between GABRIEL and JOSAPHAT, they move stage left.

JEAN-MARC:
Be careful, it's very steep. There used to be a catwalk that went out from somewhere around here, and at the end, there was a well, there was a rope that hung down, with a pulley and a bucket. So when you went to fetch water, instead of leaning over a black hole, you leaned over this pit full of light and branches, and at the bottom, a creek that reflected the sky . . . It was like . . . the opposite of a well. You see what I mean, you'd walk through the air to get water. So, we used

to call it the suspended well . . . For a kid from the city, it was really something . . .

MATHIEU:
    We should build a new one. Good Lord, listen to me, I talk as if we're gonna stay here for the rest of our lives . . .

JEAN-MARC:
    You probably can't drink the water now anyway . . .

LA GROSSE FEMME: *(off)*
    What do we do with the bottle of milk? It's awfully hot in the house . . .

ÉDOUARD: *(off)*
    I'll take it down to the crique . . .

ALBERTINE: *(off)*
    Mon Dieu, you talk like moman . . .

    ÉDOUARD comes out of the house.

ÉDOUARD:
    Ouan, and I have her common sense, too . . .

ALBERTINE: *(off)*
    Ouan . . . we're lucky you don't wear her dresses, too . . .

    ÉDOUARD stops in his tracks.

ÉDOUARD: *(as if to himself)*
    Tiens, it's the first time you've ever mentioned that . . .

    He in turn steps between GABRIEL and JOSAPHAT, walks around JEAN-MARC and MATHIEU, and disappears toward the creek.

26

ÉDOUARD: *(giving himself courage)*
If I don't break my neck and if I'm not eaten by a
bear, I'll offer my soul up to God and I'll join les
Franciscains. Non, les Dominicains, they're cuter. A
little white robe would look so nice with my redhead's
complexion . . . Mon Dieu, I'm scared . . . Why
didn't I just lower the goddammed bottle by the
well . . . AYOYE!

LA GROSSE FEMME comes out of the house.

LA GROSSE FEMME:
Did you hurt yourself, Édouard?

ÉDOUARD:
Non, non, I'll never be able to have children, that's all!

*ÉDOUARD comes back as ALBERTINE comes out
of the house.*

ALBERTINE:
It's crazy, hein, I really am scared alone in the house.

ÉDOUARD:
I don't blame you! You might meet yourself in a dark corner!

*All eight of them look in the direction of the setting
sun. They hold the pose for a good, long time.*

JOSAPHAT:
They call that the sunset, but it's not the real sunset . . .

GABRIEL:
Non?

JOSAPHAT:
Non . . . You see, here we're surrounded by

27

mountains, so when the sun sets for us, it's still high for everyone else . . .

GABRIEL:
That means we get the sunset first?

JOSAPHAT:
Non, it means we never get the real sunset.

ALBERTINE, LA GROSSE FEMME and ÉDOUARD go back inside while MATHIEU and JEAN-MARC return to their chairs.

VICTOIRE:
My good man, it's time for you to go to bed.

JOSAPHAT: *(ironic)*
Who're you talking to?

VICTOIRE:
Josaphat, franchement, in front of the boy . . .

VICTOIRE, JOSAPHAT and GABRIEL are sitting on the top step of the verandah.

JEAN-MARC:
Usually, when you buy a house, you say to yourself "Ah, there are good vibes, here" . . . Sometimes it's true and sometimes it's only to convince yourself that you've made the right choice. *(He stands up.)* But, you see, when I came to look at this house in the spring, as soon as I walked in I knew this was the right place, that this house was waiting for me . . . it was the vibes of my own family that were for sale . . . I even bought it from my father's brother-in-law . . . In the hundred years that this house has stood, it's my own family that has fought here, argued here, made

peace, cried, tapped its feet, played the fiddle and the accordéon, sung songs and made up new jigs. There have been unforgettable parties, crazy funerals, an especially odd marriage, quite sad actually, that turned my grandfather into my great uncle . . . My father, my grandmother and my real grandfather sat right here, like us, tonight, but for years . . . They watched the sun go down . . . They had the same eerie feeling when darkness fell, just before the mosquitoes came out of the woods . . . Maybe they too, thought they were nothing in the middle of nothing, without knowing what lay in store for them, without knowing where they were headed . . . My mother came here to get a break from me one summer, 'cause I'd just had scarlet fever and I was unbearable; ma tante Albertine and mon oncle Édouard tried to make peace, maybe right here on the verandah . . . My cousin Marcel played with his frigging imaginary cat . . . Ma tante Madeleine was dumped here by her husband, almost every summer of their lives, while he chased women all over the Province . . . All that belongs to me, Mathieu, it's all part of my heritage, in fact, it's my only heritage. I would have bought this house even if I'd been disappointed by it after all these years; even if the roof was caving in and the porch was rotten . . . even if it had been unliveable. I bought all those memories to keep them from sinking into indifference.

MATHIEU: *(very softly)*
And to revive them?

JEAN-MARC:
If nothing else, to help me try. One summer won't be enough . . .

MATHIEU:
You sure you'll be able to spend two months here, alone?

JEAN-MARC:
Nope.

A last surge of light after the sunset sweeps the stage.

Everything is streaked with red and is a bit fantastic.

GABRIEL:
Pis toé, mon oncle Josaphat, have you ever been to Morial?

JOSAPHAT:
Have I been to Morial? Why, dozens of times! Hundreds of times!

GABRIEL:
Hein! Pas vrai!

JOSAPHAT:
As sure as I'm sitting here, mon p'tit gars! *(with a little smile)* And so have you!

GABRIEL:
I have?

JOSAPHAT:
Certainement! I never told you that?

GABRIEL: *(who can tell there is a story in the works)*
Non, never.

VICTOIRE:
You be careful what you say, Josaphat.

JOSAPHAT: *(teasingly)*
If you don't want to hear about Gabriel's trips to Morial, Victoire, you can always go back in the house . . .

VICTOIRE:
>You'll talk so loud, I'll hear you anyway! After that, it's bedtime, Gabriel.

GABRIEL:
>Ben oui, ben oui.

JOSAPHAT:
>This house behind you, Gabriel, did you ever take a good look at it? Hein? *(He takes Gabriel by the hand and places him facing the house.)* This house, mon p'tit gars, is no ordinary house! Did you ever notice how it's got something the other houses don't have? Hein?

GABRIEL:
>The upside down well with the crique below?

JOSAPHAT:
>Non, non, I don't mean what's around the house, I mean the house itself! But . . . maybe it only happens when you're asleep. *(He winks at Victoire)* Moé, I think it only happens when you're asleep . . . But I'll tell you anyway. Now listen to this . . . This house isn't set on the hill like the others are set on their land . . . You go over to 'Ti-Poil Chevrette's place, and you'd say: "Now, there's a house, plunked down in the middle of the forest, in a big hole, how can they even see in a house like that, there must not be any light . . . " or you go over to Jos Simard's, who practically lives *IN* Lac Simon, and you'd say to yourself: "They're too close to the water, that must be dangerous when the lake breaks up in the spring!" but when you stand before our house, so lovely up here on the hill, like it was on its tip-toes to see if the countryside is as beautiful as ever, you don't get the impression it's been set down on its land like the other houses . . . When you arrive from Duhamel, you can see it, floating over the pines . . . You never noticed that?

GABRIEL:
Oui, oui, you've often told me.

JOSAPHAT:
Ben, mon p'tit gars, you know why you have the impression she floats over top of the pine trees?

GABRIEL:
Non.

JOSAPHAT:
Come here . . .

They back up a few steps.

JOSAPHAT:
Look up on the roof . . . Maybe it's still too light to see it clearly . . . but . . . there's a rope that starts at the roof and climbs right up into the sky! And at the end of the rope, there's an anchor, a ship's anchor! Notre maison isn't set on the ground, Gabriel, notre maison is suspended from the end of a rope and from an anchor that's hooked into the sky! Sometimes, during the summer storms, or the snowstorms in winter, the anchor gets caught in all kinds of things, and the house shakes . . . You've felt that, haven't you, when the house shakes?

GABRIEL: *(not too sure of himself)*
Ben oui!

JOSAPHAT:
Why just last week, we found you hiding in the closet after that big storm, because you were afraid the house would come crashing down around you like a house-of-cards . . . Well, you needn't worry, mon p'tit gars, this house will never collapse because it's held together

from up there! And the anchor's solid! There's nothing as solid as the sky. *(Silence. Then a change of tone.)* And sometimes, like at the end of the week, when there's a square dance at ma tante Blanche's place, in St-Jérôme, or chez ma tante Ozéa in Morial . . . You know what I do? You won't believe it . . . listen to this, mon p'tit gars . . . I come out onto the verandah with my fiddle, I sit down in my chair, I face towards the north . . . and I start to play "The Jig for the Devil on Vacation", tapping my feet and making as much noise as possible! I want them to hear me loud and clear, you understand?

GABRIEL:
Who's that?

JOSAPHAT:
You know, I already told you about them. The fellas who sell their souls to the devil so they can have a drink or a woman at the end of the week.

VICTOIRE:
Josaphat, he's only eleven . . .

JOSAPHAT: *(carried away by his own story)*
The ones in la Chasse-Galerie, the outcasts, the damned, who've gone crazy with cabin fever and who'll do anything for a bit of fun . . . Sometimes I have to play for a long time, but sooner or later, I hear them coming from far off . . . I see their canoe rise up behind the mountain at the end of Lac Simon, a beautiful big canoe that sails through the sky with six men who paddle as they go and who sing to each other to give themselves courage . . . They weave around the clouds, they pass in front of the moon, waving to her as they go by . . . Me, I jump up and down on the verandah, I whistle at them, I wave my arms and my

33

fiddle . . . They turn this way, they draw nearer . . . and there they are!

GABRIEL:
There they are!

JOSAPHAT:
"What do you want?" they ask, with the big voices of men who've had too much to drink . . . "I have to play at a dance tonight and it's too far to go in a buggy!" And you know what, Gabriel, you won't believe this but I swear it's the truth; the boys take the ship's anchor, they hook it onto their canoe . . . and they head off . . . At first, they have a hard time, I mean, you know, it's stuck . . . They say: "Voyons-donc, qu'est-ce qui se passe, I'm awful heavy all of a sudden . . . " They pull, and they pull . . . They strain on their paddles in the sky . . . Tu comprends, a house, it's a pretty heavy thing to pull!

VICTOIRE: *(ironically)*
Especially for a canoe . . .

JOSAPHAT:
Then suddenly, she cracks loose, she breaks away, she comes free and the canoe sails away . . . and the house rises up into the sky, carried off by the canoe!

VICTOIRE:
Josaphat, franchement!

JOSAPHAT:
And off we all go to ma tante Blanche, or to ma tante Ozéa! The forest slides away beneath us, Duhamel is tout petit, les Laurentides disappear completely into the darkness . . . The house sways gently . . . Me and your mother, we just sit here on the verandah and

watch the sky go by. Usually all we see from here is a big black hole where Lac Simon is, but now it's the Big Dipper, the Little Dipper, la planète Mars . . . The house turns on the end of the rope and we see the whole sky pass before us, like la parade on St-Jean-Baptiste Day. During the whole journey, the house sways gently back and forth, back and forth . . . Us, we're sitting pretty. It sure is beautiful. *(Silence. The three characters look around them.)* When we get to our relatives', the canoe sets us down next to their place, bonsoir la compagnie, get out your accordéons, push the chairs against the wall, here we are! And then, let me tell you, the party starts in earnest! *(He dances en turlutant, then stops as if at the end of a story.)* And that, mon p'tit gars, is how you've been to Morial without even realizing!

GABRIEL: *(on the verge of tears)*
Why don't you wake me up! I'd like to see all that, too!

JOSAPHAT remains stuck, but only for a few seconds.

JOSAPHAT:
Ben . . . We do! Lots of times! But you're too sound asleep! You can't stay awake! You know what you're like, you sleep like a log! We wake you, you get up, you go have a pee, you say bonsoir to ma tante Blanche or to ma tante Ozéa, and you go back to bed . . . The next morning, you say "I dreamt of ma tante Blanche" or "ma tante Ozéa . . ." but nous autres, your mother and me, we know it was no dream! But if we told you, you wouldn't believe us!

VICTOIRE:
Bon, ben, while we're waiting for the devil to come take the house away, it's time for bed, Gabriel . . .

GABRIEL:
But how do we get back?

VICTOIRE: *(tongue in cheek)*
Ouan, how do we get back, Josaphat?

JOSAPHAT:
Ah, euh . . . The same way! Exactly the same way! I tell the fella who steers the canoe, you know the one I mean, the one with the cloven hooves, I tell him when to meet us, and he comes by to fetch us just before sun-up . . .

VICTOIRE:
Bon, that's enough, he's gonna have bad dreams . . .

GABRIEL:
Are they coming for us tonight? If they come for us tonight, I won't fall asleep, that way I can sit on the verandah with you.

VICTOIRE:
Bon, tu vois . . .

JOSAPHAT:
Non, non, non . . . They won't come tonight . . . It's not even the week-end . . . Besides . . . euh, they don't come anymore . . . they haven't for a while . . . Not since the time we almost didn't make it back!

GABRIEL:
Hein! We almost didn't get back!

VICTOIRE:
Josaphat!

JOSAPHAT:
> The last time . . . Believe it or not, the last time . . .
> it doesn't happen too often, but the one with the funny
> feet, he had a bit too much to drink . . . and he forgot
> us! The three of us, we were stuck in Morial with the
> house and everything!

> *VICTOIRE looks perplexed wondering how
> JOSAPHAT will get out of this one.*

JOSAPHAT:
> I didn't know what to do! Aie, there we were in
> Morial, right on la rue des Fortifications, folks were
> about to wake up to go to Mass, and they were gonna
> find a house from the country, square in the middle of
> ma tanta Ozéa's backyard! I had to do something!

> *JOSAPHAT is fishing for words.*

VICTOIRE:
> Now you're stuck, hein? You can't get out of this one . . .

JOSAPHAT:
> You know what I did?

> *He is playing for time.*

> You know what I did?

GABRIEL:
> Non . . .

> *JOSAPHAT seems to have found something and he
> dances a few steps of a jig.*

JOSAPHAT:
> You know what I did? There must have been . . . oh

thirty or forty of us in the house . . . It was a big, big soirée . . . Ben, I made everyone get down on their knees . . . tout le monde . . . me, your mother, ma tante Ozéa, mon oncle Tancrède, all the other guests, the whole gang . . . and we called up . . . our guardian angels!

VICTOIRE and GABRIEL:
Hein!

JOSAPHAT:
Oui, oui, oui, we called up our guardian angels, real, real hard, you know, by promising them all kinds of stuff, like we wouldn't sin anymore, we'd do our Easter Duty, ten times a year, and we'd never touch another drop of whisky til the next time . . . Me, I even swore I'd cut the rope that goes to the anchor that holds up our house so the maudit canoe wouldn't get hooked anymore! Had to be pretty desperate, hein?

VICTOIRE: *(mockingly)*
And did the angels turn up?

JOSAPHAT:
Did they turn up! Thirty or forty guardian angels, even yours, Gabriel, mind you he was half asleep, but thirty or forty beautiful guardian angels all showed up, in a nice straight line and singing hymns. They asked me what was the problem and I told them . . . *(Silence)* You know, when you're in the woods and a flock of birds all takes off at once 'cause they've been startled . . . Well, our guardian angels . . . they went outside . . . they asked us to close our eyes . . . and we heard . . . this enormous rush of wings . . . as if they weren't forty anymore . . . but forty thousand . . . the sound of forty thousand wings rising up in the sky over Morial. It was unbelievable . . . And me . . . you

know me . . . I opened one eye . . . then the other . . .
I crept over to the window . . . All I could see was
white, moving faster and faster . . . A tornado of
white feathers surrounded the house . . . The house
shook a bit . . . But it wasn't curses and drinking
songs that we heard . . . it was hymns coming straight
from Heaven . . . The house rose gently into the sky,
and that day, for once, it wasn't the devil who brought
us home to Duhamel!

GABRIEL: *(saddened)*
Did you have to cut the rope?

JOSAPHAT:
Are you crazy?

GABRIEL is delighted.

VICTOIRE shakes her head.

VICTOIRE:
Maudit charmer . . .

JOSAPHAT: *(taking a deep bow)*
Charmer to the end of time . . . For you, Victoire, and
for you, my boy . . .

VICTOIRE: *(troubled)*
Say good night to mon oncle Josaphat, Gabriel . . . and
give him a kiss for his lovely story . . .

*JOSAPHAT picks up GABRIEL and holds him up in
his arms.*

JOSAPHAT:
Would you like me to hang you up in the sky too? With
a little anchor? You'd swing back and forth next to the
house . . . and you'd be éternel!

He kisses GABRIEL and hands him his fiddle to carry inside.

They are in darkness.

We can distinguish their silhouettes. VICTOIRE and GABRIEL go into the house; JOSAPHAT remains standing on the verandah.

The wail of a fiddle.

We hear a loud scream from in the house, the door bursts open.
ALBERTINE comes rushing out, followed by ÉDOUARD, in a dressing gown and curlers.

ALBERTINE:
Maudit fou, you scared me half to death! I thought it was our belle-soeur coming into my room . . .

ÉDOUARD: *(laughing)*
I couldn't wait to try it! I prepared it weeks ago . . . I borrowed her old night gown, I stuck a few rollers under a hair net . . . et voilà, un miracle . . . Another brilliant creation by the talented Édouard! I knew you'd think it was her!

ALBERTINE:
Aie, we haven't been here two hours and I've already been scared twelve times . . . I'm exhausted!

ÉDOUARD:
Okay, but we're on vacation, Bartine . . . We've gotta laugh a little . . .

ALBERTINE:
You two are on vacation, not me! Maybe I'd like to

laugh, too, but you never stop laughing at me! So what am I supposed to do, stand in front of my mirror and laugh? Sorry, but I didn't prepare a bunch of jokes . . . Maybe you think I'm boring, but to me, being on vacation doesn't mean dressing up like our belle-soeur to scare people . . . Ah, go and change, you look ridiculous . . . It's as if I'm not even talking to you . . .

ÉDOUARD:
Pretend it's her, maybe it'll be easier . . .

ALBERTINE:
What's that supposed to mean?

ÉDOUARD:
It means what it means, that's all . . . Whenever you and I talk, she's always there . . . that is we make sure she's there . . . and it's as if we only spoke to her . . . We don't look at one another when we talk, we look at her . . . Look, we even brought her on vacation with us . . . as if we were afraid to talk directly to each other.

ALBERTINE:
If we don't talk directly to each other, maybe it's because we've nothing to say.

ÉDOUARD:
I don't see how that can be, a brother and sister who've nothing to say . . .

ALBERTINE:
What do you expect, when one of them's not normal . . .

ÉDOUARD:
It's true, I'd forgotten you're not normal . . .

41

ALBERTINE:
I was talking about you!

ÉDOUARD:
Believe it or not, I'd figured that out! Your sense of humour, Bartine, will always amaze me!

ALBERTINE:
In any case, if our belle-soeur hadn't come with us, I wouldn't have come either! To tell you the truth, the thought of a week alone with you makes me sick!

She goes into the house.

ÉDOUARD:
Some day, I'm gonna slug her . . .

LA GROSSE FEMME slips outside.

LA GROSSE FEMME:
Really and truly, I feel like a spy. I was there, hiding behind the door . . .

ÉDOUARD:
I hope she didn't see you when she went in . . .

LA GROSSE FEMME:
I think she's had enough shocks for one day.

ÉDOUARD:
We're off to a bad start, hein?

LA GROSSE FEMME:
It doesn't look promising, non.

ÉDOUARD:
Why am I so clumsy with her? I can't seem to get near her . . .

LA GROSSE FEMME:
Ah, ça, no one can do that . . .

ÉDOUARD:
You know how to talk to her . . . How do you do it?

LA GROSSE FEMME:
After so many years, living in the same house . . . I
guess I've just learned . . . when to leave her
alone . . . I've learned not to argue with her . . .

Silence.

LA GROSSE FEMME laughs softly.

ÉDOUARD:
Why are you laughing?

LA GROSSE FEMME:
It's true, you do look like me . . .

He approaches her.

ÉDOUARD:
Next Hallowe'en, for the party at the French Casino,
we should go as twin sisters . . .

LA GROSSE FEMME:
Or twin brothers.

ÉDOUARD:
Non, non, sisters . . . dressing up as a man's no
fun . . .

LA GROSSE FEMME:
It might be fun for me . . .

ÉDOUARD:

Aie, I know! We'll go as twins, but you as a fella and me as a girl!

LA GROSSE FEMME:

You get too carried away . . . I've never set foot in the French Casino, Édouard, I'm not gonna start now, just to make you happy . . . Especially not dressed as a man for a Hallowe'en party!

ÉDOUARD:

Come on, I can just see the look on their faces . . .

LA GROSSE FEMME:

What little I know about the French Casino is what you've told me, Édouard. That's enough for me, thanks!

ALBERTINE storms out, furious.

ALBERTINE:

That's right. Sneak out so you can talk behind my back! *(She stops suddenly.)* Mon Dieu, which is which, it's so dark I can't tell you apart . . . You're really sick, hein, the two of you!

She goes back into the house.

ÉDOUARD:

I guess we'd better go in . . .

LA GROSSE FEMME:

There are no mosquitoes yet, I'm going to sit on the verandah for a while.

ÉDOUARD:

You're right. It's too early to go to bed. I'll try to get Bartine to come out.

LA GROSSE FEMME:
And light more lamps . . . It's true, with no lights on, this house is gloomy at night . . .

ÉDOUARD: *(in a falsetto voice)*
Bartine, it's me coming in, your belle-soeur . . . We'll have a nice chat . . . I know how you love to talk!

Silence.

JOSAPHAT lights his pipe.

LA GROSSE FEMME:
You can smell the water from here.

MATHIEU:
I don't want to be a drag, but you know, it's too bad to think by tomorrow, we won't be able to smell the water or the pine trees anymore . . . I want to hang on to those smells, all week long . . . You arrive, it smells great, really strong . . . and two hours later you can't smell a thing . . . It makes you want to go away and come back . . . just so you can smell it again . . .

LA GROSSE FEMME and MATHIEU take a deep breath.

JOSAPHAT: *(he turns toward the house)*
Victoire, I've got to talk to you.

LA GROSSE FEMME: *(loudly)*
Are you coming?

The door opens. SÉBASTIEN comes out.

SÉBASTIEN:
Nine-thirty! I did as you said, I turned off the TV.

45

MATHIEU:
Good for you. Did you brush your teeth?

SÉBASTIEN:
I said I turned off the TV, I didn't say I was going to bed!

MATHIEU:
Well, it's time . . .

SÉBASTIEN:
We're on vacation . . .

MATHIEU:
In any case, you're tired . . . When you rub your eyes like that, it's time for bed . . .

SÉBASTIEN:
Ah, papa . . . Stop, you're tickling me!

MATHIEU:
I am not! You'd like me to tickle you . . . to get you all wound up so you can say later it's my fault you can't sleep . . . Hein? You can't fool me . . . Anything to gain time . . .

JEAN-MARC:
Let him keep company with us for a while . . .

MATHIEU:
My God . . . "Keep company" . . . I haven't heard that for ages . . .

JEAN-MARC:
I don't know why I said that . . .

MATHIEU:
As long as you don't start talking like: "Back in my time, my boy . . ."

JEAN-MARC:
Maybe it's the house, it rubs off on me . . .

SÉBASTIEN:
Oh, I had an idea a while ago . . .

MATHIEU:
Don't interrupt when grown-ups are talking, Sébastien, how many times do I have to tell you?

SÉBASTIEN:
I didn't interrupt . . . He'd finished . . . Hein, Jean-Marc?

JEAN-MARC:
That's right, it's you who interrupted him, Mathieu . . .

MATHIEU:
I beg your pardon . . .

JEAN-MARC:
What were you going to say, Sébastien?

SÉBASTIEN:
While I was playing with the Nintendo, I had this great idea . . . I think I'll invent one of my own . . .

JEAN-MARC:
Your own what?

SÉBASTIEN:
Video game, what else? The ones I have, I know by heart . . . and the ones you rent are boring . . . It'd be fun to have a game of my own . . . I'm sick of all those knights and ladies and mazes . . . It'll take place at school . . . in the school yard. There'll be a bad kid who's always picking on the others and a good kid

47

who'll stand up for his friends . . . and to beat the bad guy, the good one will have to get through all kinds of dangers . . . Then, at the end . . .

MATHIEU: *(laughing)*
That's a great idea . . . You can start tomorrow morning . . . We've brought tons of stuff to draw with.

JEAN-MARC:
I'll help you . . .

SÉBASTIEN:
Non, non, I don't need any help . . . Well, maybe for the French, when I have to write the instruction book . . .

JEAN-MARC and MATHIEU laugh discretely.

MATHIEU:
Okay, we'll talk more about this tomorrow . . . Meanwhile, it's good night kisses, pyjamas, beddy-bye and no tickling . . . À demain.

Good night kisses all around.

SÉBASTIEN and JEAN-MARC:
À demain.

MATHIEU:
Do you want me to tuck you in?

SÉBASTIEN:
I'm not a baby. *(He goes in.)* Bonne nuit.

MATHIEU:
Bonne nuit . . .

JOSAPHAT has come closer to the house.

48

JOSAPHAT:
    I love that kid so much . . .

    Silence.

MATHIEU:
    I love that kid so much, Jean-Marc . . .

JOSAPHAT:
    It almost hurts.

    MATHIEU gets up and goes down the steps of the verandah.

MATHIEU:
    It almost hurts.

JOSAPHAT:
    If I didn't hold myself back . . .

MATHIEU:
    If I didn't hold myself back, I'd devour him! *(He smiles)* It's true!

JOSAPHAT:
    I'd devour him!

MATHIEU:
    Mon enfant!

JOSAPHAT:
    Mon enfant!

MATHIEU:
    When I hear you tell stories about your family, with your uncles and aunts, and all your cousins, so much life, so much drama, and I think about Sébastien . . . I

worry that Sébastien has no family, Jean-Marc, the same way I had no family! He's my only kid and I guess it's obvious I won't have any more, hein? I'm worried that he'll feel alone with me, just like I felt alone with my mother . . . When I think of my childhood . . . I see my mother leaning over the kitchen table, telling me . . .

JOSAPHAT:
When he was little, that's what I'd do . . .

MATHIEU:
"Finish your milk, it makes you grow tall . . . "

JOSAPHAT:
I'd devour him, from head to toe . . . I'd bite his bum when I changed his diapers, I'd bite his feet when I gave him his bath, I'd blow raspberries on his tummy . . .

MATHIEU:
It's ten past eight in the morning . . . It's time to leave for school and I don't feel like it . . . My mother has already left . . . She had to take three buses to get to work . . .

JOSAPHAT:
He always wanted me to take care of him . . .

MATHIEU:
My mother was a saint, Jean-Marc, and no one ever knew it! *(Silence.)* The two of us lived alone for years, while she struggled to give me a decent up-bringing, and me . . .

JOSAPHAT:
There was no one else in the world but mon oncle Josaphat . . .

MATHIEU:

When I was a kid, my greatest fantasy was to have a huge family, like yours. I'd make up brothers and sisters, I'd multiply the rooms in the house . . . I made up a father, too . . . a father who was present and who loved me. A prince charming of a father, who I loved . . . like I love my kid, today . . . to the point where I could eat him. I couldn't understand why my mother had dumped my father to bring me up alone in a three bedroom apartment . . .

JOSAPHAT:

And I want to go on taking care of him like I always have. Take him fishing on Lac Simon in the summer, pretend to hunt moose in the fall, because neither of us likes to kill animals . . . Tell him endless stories, stories about devils and birchbark canoes, werewolves who prowl around the house 'cause I know they don't scare him and they make him dream. I'd like to watch him grow up, become a man, and some day be able to tell him . . .

MATHIEU:

Each member of my imaginary family had a name. I'd talk with them, argue with them, fight with them, then afterwards we'd have a good cry and fall into each other's arms. I drove my mother nuts with what she called my crazy ideas . . . But I needed all that to survive! There's nothing worse in the world, Jean-Marc, than being a single child!

He looks toward the house.

JOSAPHAT:

And someday be able to tell him!

51

MATHIEU:

> When I first met you and I realized that all this actually had existed, and how important it was to you, I resented you, Jean-Marc. For having lived my dream . . . or having these collective memories, memories that go back to the beginning of the century . . . for having so many stories to tell . . . I had nothing to tell you about my family . . . My family has no memory. There is no maison suspendue in my life. And I only have one kid. Like my mother. It's true, at the time I thought I'd have more . . . Louise and I were hardly going to stop at one . . . We were going to . . . I don't know, re-populate Québec all by ourselves . . . My God. All that's in another life. My marriage is in another life. It's funny, I'm really happy for the first time in my life, but I'm afraid. For my kid. Because like my mother, I won't have given him a family. Or anything to remember. I'm afraid that I'll be happy at his expense.

JEAN-MARC:

> He has a family, with his mother, his step-father, his half-sister . . .

MATHIEU: *(blurting out)*

> Jean-Marc, if you only knew how jealous I am of them! When Sébastien sits down to eat his cereal in the morning, he has a father next to him and a baby sister . . . and I'm not there! I want him to live all that with me!

> *They both come back up onto the verandah, MATHIEU near JEAN-MARC, JOSAPHAT on the opposite end.*

JOSAPHAT:

> But why hash all that over again . . . We're probably going to move to the city, he's going to find a father

who'll bring him up like a true child, a family, a normal
life . . . *(Silence.)* I know how to make the moon
come up every night, but I can't even keep my own child!

MATHIEU:
Sorry. I'm okay.

JEAN-MARC:
Do you want to go in?

MATHIEU:
Non, non, it's nice out here. Besides, I won't sleep.

JOSAPHAT starts howling like a wolf.
VICTOIRE comes out.

MATHIEU:
Did you hear that? Are there wolves around here?

JEAN-MARC:
It's the first time I've heard that . . .

VICTOIRE:
Josaphat, you'll wake the boy!

JOSAPHAT:
Ben non, It's to help him dream . . .

MATHIEU:
I'd like his life to be full of my presence, you know
what I mean? And when he is with me, all I manage to
do is be aggressive. Instead of giving him my love, of
showering him with affection, too often I hold myself
back, and I'm too impatient. I say no to everything . . .
I get all in a huff. Yet, there's nothing I love more than
to hear him laugh! At times, he's in his room, watching
TV or playing with the goddammed Nintendo, everything

is quiet, he's concentrating, and all of a sudden his laugh rings through the whole house . . . It's so . . . so real! It's a laugh without problems, without doubts, it's a laugh for the pure pleasure of laughing! You can't imagine what that does for me, Jean-Marc . . . If I didn't always hold myself back, I'd run to his room and I'd tell him: "Don't stop, don't ever stop laughing, Sébastien, laugh, it helps me to live!" But I can't bring myself to do that. I love him so much I could devour him, but I hold back too much with him. I hold myself back too much, I hold back too much . . . Aie, we're badly made, aren't we . . .

JOSAPHAT:
Come sit with me for a bit . . .

VICTOIRE:
Le p'tit, he's not asleep yet . . .

JOSAPHAT:
We won't make any noise . . . I just want you near me.

VICTOIRE approaches JOSAPHAT. He puts his arm around her waist. She leans against him.

JOSAPHAT:
A beautiful night like this, you have to look it straight in the eye . . .

VICTOIRE: *(in desperation)*
What do they look at in the city, Josaphat, on a beautiful night like this?
The smokestacks in the factories?

LA GROSSE FEMME:
We're badly made, hein? In the city, I break my neck every night during the summer, to see the stars from

54

my balcony. I count them, I try to spot the Big Dipper, and the Little Dipper, like mon oncle Josaphat showed me, before Gabriel and I were even married . . . and when I find them, I get all excited . . . I go down onto the sidewalk, sometimes I even stand in the middle of the street to see them better . . . There they are and I think: they look at me just as I look at them . . . and I feel reassured. But when I get out here . . . On the first night, I'm always afraid to look at the sky . . . Once the sun has gone down, it's as if I were afraid to look higher than the mountain tops . . . I don't know why, there's nothing to see down below. Nothing but a black hole and the yellow ribbon of the road to Duhamel. That's all. Non, what's really beautiful is up above. But I'm afraid. Because it's too much. There are too many stars here, it frightens me. In the city, we can always imagine they're just tiny golden nails tacked to a black velvet curtain, or we can imagine nothing at all because we're too busy. You look at it and you say it's beautiful, all the while thinking about the three meals for tomorrow, the washing, the ironing . . . A woman standing in the middle of la rue Fabre counting stars and thinking of tomorrow's meals, that's me in the city. But out here . . . *(She suddenly raises her eyes to the sky, almost involuntarily)* Ah! I can't stand it, it's too much! They smother me! But still, it's so beautiful! It's not just a sprinkling of little golden nails here and there, like in the city . . . There are . . . millions . . . There are so many, you can't even find the ones you know anymore . . . There are . . . whole rivers of stars from one end of the sky to the other . . . and they seem so close, I have the impression that if I lifted my arm . . . and I gave a little flick with my hand . . . everything would start to spin . . . It's crazy, hein? As if I could make the world turn all by myself! But folks who live here, folks who spend their lives out here, aren't they scared to death under a sky like that? Do they not see it anymore, like we stop hearing the noise in the city? *(She twists her neck a bit more.)* Why are there so many? Why isn't it like when we were small and we thought the world was simple? All this is too complicated! All that clockwork, what good is it? What business do I have here if all that really exists? There is no way that all that can be looking at me.

JOSAPHAT:
If we stay up til dawn . . .

VICTOIRE:
Yeah, yeah, I know . . . If we stay up til dawn, we'll see Haley's Comet.

JOSAPHAT:
You don't care about that? If we miss it, we won't see it again for seventy-five years! We'll be one hundred and something, blind as bats, and we'll say to one another . . . "Ah, if only we'd stayed up that night . . . "

She looks at him.

VICTOIRE:
These days, there are more important things in our life than Haley's Comet, Josaphat . . .

LA GROSSE FEMME gets up, goes down the stairs, walks a few steps and stops.

LA GROSSE FEMME:
When I stand here, I'm not the same as I am in the city, because in the city nothing else exists, whereas here, I have the impression it's me who doesn't exist. *(She raises her arms to the sky.)* Why should I

exist if there's all that? Only to raise a family? Only to raise a family? The only reason I exist is to raise a family?

ÉDOUARD and ALBERTINE bring their chairs out of the house.

ALBERTINE:
I told you, I'm not gonna talk to you til you get changed.

ÉDOUARD:
And I told you, I'm not gonna get changed til I see you laugh!

ALBERTINE:
Then you're gonna stay dressed like that for the rest of your days!

LA GROSSE FEMME:
Bon, here come the two marvels . . .

ALBERTINE:
You tell him, there's no way he can stay dressed like that!

LA GROSSE FEMME:
I can barely see him, in the dark.

ALBERTINE:
It's not true, his night gown's so pale, that's all you can see! All I can see is the two of you . . . You glow in the dark, both of you, with your magnificent night gowns; it's a regular fireworks display.

LA GROSSE FEMME:
Look a bit higher, that's all.

ALBERTINE:
Hein?

LA GROSSE FEMME:
Look at the sky, it's much more interesting.

ALBERTINE lifts her head for a brief moment.

ALBERTINE:
Mon Dieu, what a lot of stars, have they added more since last night? *(To Édouard)* Just don't put your chair too close to mine . . .

ÉDOUARD:
You don't like my perfume?

ALBERTINE:
Don't tell me you put perfume on before you go to bed!

ÉDOUARD and LA GROSSE FEMME look at one another in despair.

ÉDOUARD:
To make that laugh would be like getting the fat lady in the fun house at Parc Belmont, to cry . . .

LA GROSSE FEMME:
At least the fat lady at Parc Belmont is plugged in . . .

ÉDOUARD: *(lifting his sister's skirt)*
Oh, have you come unplugged, Bartine?

ALBERTINE:
Get your hands away from there!

ÉDOUARD:
For all there is to see . . .

ALBERTINE:
We know you're not interested anyway, so don't be a smart aleck!

ÉDOUARD:
That's twice you've mentioned that tonight . . .

ALBERTINE: *(defiantly)*
Mentioned what?

ÉDOUARD:
You really want to talk about it?

ALBERTINE stares him down for a few seconds then looks away.

ÉDOUARD:
That's what I thought . . .

LA GROSSE FEMME comes back and sits down on the top step.

ÉDOUARD:
Take my chair . . .

LA GROSSE FEMME:
Non, non . . .

ÉDOUARD:
Let me get you one in the house . . .

LA GROSSE FEMME:
Non, laisse-faire, I'm fine here . . . In the city, I'd look like a real nut sitting on the ground, but here it doesn't matter . . . no one else can see us . . . and it makes me feel young again . . .

ALBERTINE:
If that's all it takes to make you feel young, you're
damn lucky . . .

LA GROSSE FEMME:
What I mean is, I often used to sit here with Gabriel,
when I was younger, . . .

ÉDOUARD:
That's right, you came here on your honeymoon . . .
Aie, you were a long way from Niagara Falls,
hein . . . I guess you had nothing else to do but to . . .

ALBERTINE:
Édouard, franchement!

LA GROSSE FEMME:
You're right, and that's about all we did, too . . .

> *She smiles.*
> *Brief silence.*
> *JOSAPHAT lets out a little wolf howl.*
> *VICTOIRE pokes him with her elbow.*

ALBERTINE:
Would someone tell me why, for the love of God,
we're out here on the verandah? There's nothing to
see! It's black as pitch! We came out to look at
nothing?

ÉDOUARD:
Bartine, franchement! T'es choquante! I know you lack
fantasy and imagination, but there's a limit! If you don't
see anything, pretend you do, or close your eyes and
take a big whiff, don't tell me you can't smell anything,
for God's sake, it smells so good it's almost hard to
breathe! We came here for a rest, relax!

ALBERTINE:
How can I relax with my brother sitting next to me, dressed like a scarecrow!

LA GROSSE FEMME:
Thanks a lot!

ALBERTINE:
In the city, you drive me nuts every time you come through the door, because we never know what's in store for us, and here I've come to spend a week with you in the country, I must be out of my mind!

ÉDOUARD:
All three of us needed a rest . . .

ALBERTINE:
Did we need to rest together?

ÉDOUARD:
Maudit, que t'es bête! This is the only place in the country where we can go, Grumpy!

ALBERTINE gets up, furious.

ALBERTINE:
I had no wish to come here! I have bad memories of this place, it's not my fault! I have bad memories of this verandah, and I'm sure as hell not gonna spend a week sitting on it! I've already seen the sky! I tried to drown my rage in it and it didn't work, I'm not about to try again just to please you!

LA GROSSE FEMME:
Not so loud, you'll wake up le p'tit . . .

ALBERTINE:
He's my kid, I'll wake him if I like!

LA GROSSE FEMME and ÉDOUARD look at one another.

ALBERTINE:
I'm sorry. You're right. We have to let children sleep. Especially that one. And if he wakes up, he'll just start with his nonsense again . . .

ÉDOUARD:
That's right, settle down . . .

LA GROSSE FEMME:
Voices carry in the country . . . They probably heard you in Duhamel.

ÉDOUARD:
They must have thought there's a bear caught in a trap . . . Come on, Bartine, laugh just a little . . . I want to go put on my pale pink silk pyjamies . . .

LA GROSSE FEMME laughs.
ALBERTINE shakes her head.

VICTOIRE:
So, do we move to Morial or non?

JOSAPHAT:
You know darn well, it's your decision.

VICTOIRE:
Sure. Sure, it's up to me.

JEAN-MARC:
So, have you decided?

MATHIEU:
What?

JEAN-MARC:
To keep Sébastien for the whole summer.

MATHIEU:
I think so. If he's game. If he wants to stay with me.

JOSAPHAT:
When do you give him a final answer?

VICTOIRE:
Who?

JOSAPHAT:
Ben, à Télesphore!

VICTOIRE:
Any day now. Any day.

MATHIEU:
You'll be out here, I don't start rehearsals til
September . . . We'll have a great time together . . .
At least, I hope so. In two months, I might learn to
live a normal life with him . . . even make up some
memories for us . . .

ALBERTINE:
Mind you, if you led a normal life, you might be easier
to talk to . . .

VICTOIRE:
Télesphore has promised me a normal life, Josaphat,
but I don't know if I want it . . .

MATHIEU:

But you, all alone, surrounded by mountains, aren't you afraid you'll die of boredom?

JEAN-MARC:

More likely, I'll die of fright! You know how chicken I am! Forty-eight and scared out of my wits by a dark night or the slightest odd noise . . . When you two leave, it'll be the first time in ages I'll have lived alone . . . Another great victory over myself . . .

MATHIEU:

Nothing can happen to you . . .

JEAN-MARC:

I know nothing can happen to me! It's not thieves I'm scared of, there's nothing here to steal! Look, some people are afraid of the dark, some people are afraid of crowds, of elevators, spiders, me, I'm afraid of being alone at night . . . It's not very original, but there you are . . . And I'm not asking you to understand . . .

MATHIEU:

Who says I don't understand? But let me point out that it's not too smart to spend a summer alone in the woods if you're scared of the Boogeyman!

JEAN-MARC:

Don't be ridiculous . . . If I were afraid of the Boogeyman, Mathieu, I could talk myself out of it . . . *(He looks around him.)* In any case, I won't know for sure til after you've left . . .

ÉDOUARD:

If I led a normal life, Bartine, I'd be the most boring person in the world. The rest of the family's boring enough.

JEAN-MARC:

I hope the bears don't still get in the garbage . . . If we've got wolves too, now I'll really be nervous . . .

JOSAPHAT:

Me, I know I don't want it, but I also know we have no choice . . .

ÉDOUARD:

Call me what you will, you can't say I'm boring!

ALBERTINE:

You're not boring, you're frightening!

MATHIEU: *(smiling)*

So what will you do to get over your fear? Live at night and sleep all day? For a writer, talk about clichés . . .

VICTOIRE:

I'm afraid, Josaphat, that either way I'll make the wrong choice . . .

JEAN-MARC gets up and goes down the steps, brushing against his mother.

JEAN-MARC:

In any case, if it's going to happen, it'll happen here, hein? By the end of the summer, I'll know on the one hand if I'm still afraid of the dark, and on the other if I can make this house live again.

ÉDOUARD also gets up and goes down the steps.

ÉDOUARD:

I don't do anything like other people, Bartine, nothing, and boy do I love being the only one to do what I do!

Right now, I have to go fetch some water, because we'll need it tomorrow morning; Baby, I'll get that water like no one in Duhamel has ever fetched water before! Sure, you think that to fetch water is so boring you could die with your mouth open? Well, me, I'm going to make it so exciting! That's my strength, Bartine.

He strikes a dramatic pose and begins reciting "Le Songe d'Athalie" (Racine), as he heads for the well.

ÉDOUARD:
C'était pendant l'horrreuur d'une profonde nuit,
Ma mèèère Jézabél devant moi s'est montréeuh
Comme aux juuurs de sa mort pompeusement paréeuh . . .

He goes out.

ÉDOUARD: *(in mid-verse)*
Jesus Christ it's dark!

LA GROSSE FEMME laughs.

ALBERTINE:
You think that's funny, do you?

LA GROSSE FEMME:
If you didn't know him, if he wasn't your brother, you'd laugh, too . . .

ALBERTINE:
If he wasn't my brother, I wouldn't be ashamed . . .

MATHIEU:
Jean-Marc, will you ever really talk to me?

66

JEAN-MARC:
>What do you mean?

MATHIEU:
>You know what I mean. You'd been saying for so long you were going to quit teaching, I thought you'd never do it. That you'd never have the guts. Then, all of a sudden, you do it without warning . . . You come home with the news as if it were no big deal, and you're surprised that I'm surprised . . . You're no longer a professor, and you're going to spend the summer in your family's house which you've just bought . . . and where you might die of fright because you're scared of being alone . . . On the one hand you do all you can to be alone, and on the other, you're afraid . . . And I'm supposed to blend right in . . . I'm not always prepared for you, Jean-Marc . . . I don't understand your actions because you don't talk about them enough. Everything gets bottled up but nothing ever comes out. At times, I have the impression I know your family better than I do you. You reveal yourself in dribs and drabs, which aren't always clear, but you talk about the others for hours on end . . . so much so . . . so much that we know them, we see them, we live with them, even though they've been dead for ages . . .

>*ÉDOUARD comes back with a bucket of water that he carries with both hands.*

ÉDOUARD:
>Ouf! Mademoiselle Athalie isn't quite so glamorous, now! In fact, she's sweating like a pig!

ALBERTINE:
>You've got too much water, it's spilling over . . .

ÉDOUARD:
Aie, you want me to take some back?

ALBERTINE:
Yes, and stay there while you're at it . . .

He goes up the steps and turns around before going into the house.

ÉDOUARD:
After her triumphant performance in "La Porteuse de pain", you can see la Duchesse de Langeais in "Manon des Sources" wiss za axang de Marseilla puis touta . . . Un grand moment de théâtre! In four acts and thirty-two buckets; count them!

He goes into the house.

ALBERTINE:
You think that's funny, too?

LA GROSSE FEMME: *(wiping her eyes)*
So do you, Bartine, I know you do . . .

MATHIEU:
Sometimes, I have to wade through that whole crowd to reach you, and I get discouraged. They're like a fence between us, and most of the time they're a pain in the ass . . .

JEAN-MARC:
I don't know, Mathieu, if I've really left teaching or if . . . *(Silence.)* Up until recently, when I'd see one of my colleagues, a little older than me, get his inevitable but questionable sabbatical, I'd say: "Ah, voilà, another who's found an excuse for living off society for a year!" I'd watch them go off, all smiles,

as if their prison door had opened after twenty years of hard labour; at times I'd get a postcard from some place I'd never heard of, at times I'd hear they were just shut up in the house, depressed or paranoid, and, when the year was up, I'd watch them come back more depressed than ever because now they had to start all over again, as if that year had never existed . . . And naïvely I'd tell myself I'd never do that because I love my profession, because my students inspire me and never in a million years would I need to get away from it all . . . And here I am . . . You begin your career with enthusiasm, you're going to shape people's lives, you have a responsibility . . . If the teachers who preceded you bored their students, you won't make their mistake, non, you will make them passionate because you are passionate yourself! How long does it last, seven, eight years . . . And by sheer repetition, the same things year after year, the same course, you become so sick of it you start hating the students as much as your subject! You don't need to prepare your course anymore, you know it too well, you've *become* your course. You've become the king of bullshit! You look for new ways to say the same goddammed things and there aren't any! You've tried them all! You're like an actor who has played the same part all his life and who ends up hating it. So, before you kill one of your students, or sink into a deep depression, you start dreaming . . . of a year's vacation, at the university's expense because it owes you that much after fifteen or twenty years of playing the trained parrot . . . You've become bitter, nasty, like the older profs you despised when you began . . . I loved my profession so much, Mathieu, and now I hate it with a passion!

ÉDOUARD comes out of the house. He is dressed in rather startling pale pink silk pyjamas.

69

ALBERTINE:
Mon Dieu, that's all we needed! They really do exist, those pink pyjamas!

ÉDOUARD:
Tu comprends, the basic element of any wardrobe worthy of the name is an attractive pair of pyjamas which lays the ground for all assaults, and even provokes them!

JEAN-MARC:
But instead of running off to some obscure corner of the world to send idiotic postcards to my friends, I decided to withdraw into this corner of my childhood . . . to try and bring back to life the pink pyjamas of mon oncle Édouard, the rage of ma tante Albertine, the doubts and hesitations of my grandmother, the desperation of my grandfather, the intelligence of my mother . . . *(A sudden shift in light. The door to the house opens, out comes Marcel, carrying the bird cage.)* and the imagination of my cousin, Marcel.

MARCEL:
Viens, Duplessis . . . They're all asleep . . . *(He sets down the cage and opens the little door.)* Don't be afraid, there's no danger . . . This is what you call the country . . . *(He sits next to the cage.)* C'est ça . . . you can explore all you want . . . but don't wander off, I'll be worried . . . Viens, viens me voir . . . don't go too far, come here . . . c'est ça, come to me . . . You're too beautiful,Duplessis . . . you're too beautiful. *(He caresses the invisible cat.)* We'll be fine, here, just the two of us . . . You can teach me all there is to know, and me, I'll caress you . . . *(He lies on his back.)* You're tickling me, Duplessis, your whiskers are tickling me . . . *(He*

laughs.) Climb on my tummy . . . c'est ça . . . lie
down on my tummy . . . *(He caresses Duplessis.)* On
est bien, hein? On est bien, ici . . . On est bien . . .
We're gonna be . . . happy.

ALBERTINE:
Go back inside and put on the night gown . . . It's not
as ugly . . .

MARCEL starts.

MARCEL:
That's Moman's voice . . . quick, we've gotta go
in . . . we can't let her find us here . . . Come on,
Duplessis, we've got to go in . . . we've got to go
in . . .

He picks up the cage and goes in.

JEAN MARC:
I'll give myself a year. And if I don't make it . . . *(He
goes back up the steps of the verandah and sits down.)*
But I'll never go back to the University, Mathieu,
never!

VICTOIRE:
If we leave Duhamel, Josaphat, I'll never come back,
never! Not in ten years, not in thirty . . . never! Nor
will I ever want to talk about it . . .

JOSAPHAT:
We can't help talking about where we come from,
Victoire, c'est pas possible . . .

VICTOIRE:
Ben moi, je vas être capable! If you're going to cut me

71

off from all this, if you're going to take all this away from me, afterwards you'll have to pretend it never existed! I'm warning you! And I'm going to warn Télesphore, too!

She comes down off the verandah.

VICTOIRE: *(violently)*
We were born here, Josaphat, surrounded by nature, in the back woods, on the edge of a lake, on the edge of a lake, Josaphat! We've watched it freeze over and melt for thirty years, we take our fish from it, our lives are governed by that lake! When it's frozen over, we put on our snow shoes to go to Duhamel, and when it thaws we get out the canoe . . . The sun comes up at one end of that lake and it goes down at the other, and we watch it because in front of notre maison, there's nothing to hide the sun from us as it goes up, crosses the sky and goes down! We were lucky to be born here in the country and we should stay here, that's what folks we know in the city all tell us, and the folks we know in the city left the country because they had to and now they're so miserable they could die! Our sister Ozéa, Josaphat, when she comes here, all she does is cry because she knows that when her vacation's over she'll have to go back! We're not in the magic world of la Chasse-Galerie, Josaphat, where everything is beautiful and we can travel from Morial to Duhamel in a birchbark canoe, driven by the Devil himself, whenever it suits our fancy! This is real life! And in real life, when we leave Duhamel, it's forever!

Silence.

VICTOIRE:
You've nothing to say? I'm not surprised, faced with real life, poets never have anything to say . . . They stare into the distance, and they pretend to think.

JOSAPHAT:
   Come on, be fair. I'm not pretending to think. I'm
   listening to you.

VICTOIRE:
   Ben j'ai fini, so answer me!

JOSAPHAT:
   I'll wait a bit. When you're all wound up, you're
   impossible to talk to.

ALBERTINE:
   At least we could talk! That might fill the dark.

ÉDOUARD:
   When you're all wound up, you're impossible to talk to.

ALBERTINE:
   I'm wound up every time I see you, does that mean
   we should never talk?

   She gets up, goes down the steps and joins her mother.

ALBERTINE: *(same tone as her mother)*
   You don't know what you do to me, Édouard, hein, you
   really don't know! You don't realize how everything
   you represent makes me sick! You play with me, you
   play with my reactions to your stupid nonsense, but
   you don't realize how serious it is, how really serious it
   is! When you come through the door, on Saturday
   night, for your weekly visit, and I hear your goddammed
   voice, which is never the same, I tell myself I've no
   idea who you're gonna look like this time, and all I
   want to do is run out the back door and down the alley!
   Have you ever stopped to think, Édouard, that none of
   us in the house knows who you are? We don't know!
   The other women on la rue Fabre, when they see their

73

brothers come up the street from la rue Mont-Royal, they say: tiens, v'là mon frère Émile, or v'là mon frère Albert . . . Not me! One Saturday night it's Juliette Pétrie who comes sauntering up the street, and the next Saturday, it's Shirley Temple with a dress that's too short or La Poune with her little cap . . . Sometimes it's the neighbours, Édouard, who tell me: tiens, v'là votre frère, and I want to spit in their faces because I'm afraid of whatever it is that's coming! In the winter it's not so bad . . . I don't get my surprise til you're in the kitchen and I can hide my shame in the oven, pretending to baste the roast of pork, but in the summer, Édouard, in the summer, it's the whole of la rue Fabre that sees you coming . . . I see you come up the street the same time as everyone else and there's no way I can hide my shame! The whole world can see the shame on my face! *(She screams.)* If you don't take off those ridiculous pyjamas and put on something decent, I'm going to rip them off your back and you'll have to go fish them up from the end of the dock!

She is trembling.

Silence.

ALBERTINE: *(more softly)*
If you brought me here to talk to me, and I know you brought me here to talk to me, I'm not completely stupid, do it without a disguise. We're not in the city now, we don't have to play roles, we're out in the woods, on the edge of an empty, dark lake, there's an army of mosquitoes out there just waiting for us to smell strong enough so they can eat us alive, so we might as well settle this right now, before we start to itch. *(She turns toward them.)* The two of you have trapped me here, but we'll see who's the strongest . . .

MATHIEU:

It's so calm . . . Who could imagine there'd been arguments here . . . Everything you tell me about your family seems incredible in calm like this.

JEAN-MARC:

Don't trust appearances . . . If this house could talk . . .

VICTOIRE:

If you don't talk to me, I'm going to go to bed . . . To sleep on it, as they say . . . But I'll only be sleeping on the same thing as last night and the night before that, and I'll wake up knowing what I've known all along . . .

ALBERTINE:

So, go on, talk to me, say something . . . You want to put me on trial? Fine, I'll defend myself, without a lawyer . . .

ÉDOUARD: *(applauding)*

Bravo! Belle performance! You always bring trouble on yourself, don't you? You always think that your tantrums will scare us and that we'll give in, just so you'll stop screaming! Okay, we'll do it your way again . . . I'll go in, I'll put on my nice clean little suit . . . but then, and I'm warning you, don't expect me to give in, or us to cut off the discussion because you get hysterical . . . you're going to hear me out, to the bitter end!

He goes in.

Silence.

ALBERTINE: *(to her sister-in-law)*

This was all planned in advance, hein?

LA GROSSE FEMME:
> It wasn't supposed to happen like this . . . Especially not tonight, as soon as we arrived . . .

ALBERTINE:
> In any case, I'm warning you, if this turns sour, we're leaving tomorrow morning! I'm not going through this every night . . . Non, certain!

LA GROSSE FEMME:
> Why did you come, Bartine . . .

ALBERTINE:
> Quoi?

LA GROSSE FEMME:
> Why did you let yourself be talked into coming . . . Weren't you sort of hoping all this would happen?

ALBERTINE:
> All what? Having things out with Édouard? With that big nobody who is only good at playing the buffoon? Voyons donc! Now you listen to me . . . He'll come back out here, dressed up as usual, he'll recite some poetic nonsense from a play or else he'll sing la chanson de la Poune and pretend that nothing's happened . . . He always pretends nothing's happened! You can tear strips off him, call him every name in the book, and afterwards, he doesn't remember a thing! He always slips between your fingers! He's like a bar of wet soap! My brother is a bar of wet soap! Did you ever try to talk to a bar of wet soap?

JOSAPHAT:
> In the city we won't be outcasts anymore, Victoire.

VICTOIRE:

> In the city, Josaphat, we won't be alive anymore! Do you know what life Télesphore has offered me? Do you?

> *JOSAPHAT steps down from the verandah.*

JOSAPHAT:

> Télesphore has offered to recognize Gabriel for you, Victoire, he's offered to . . . legalize Gabriel if you'll go with him to the city. Here, everybody knows, now, it's hard to even get served at the general store, at church they almost throw rocks at us . . .

VICTOIRE:

> I know that. I know, don't start that again, I know all that, it's been like that for years . . .

JOSAPHAT:

> Think of him, Gabriel . . .

VICTOIRE:

> Josaphat, Télesphore has been offered a job as janitor in an apartment house on la ruelle des Fortifications in Morial, do you think that's something we can wish for a child? Where are they going to put us, in the basement? Next to the coal bin? Gabriel, our child, the child we made, you and me, are we going to make him grow up in a basement in the city after giving him . . . *(She indicates the lake.)* all this?

JOSAPHAT: *(ashamed)*

> Télesphore told you, Victoire, it's a job, just for the time being!

VICTOIRE:

> We know about your jobs just for the time being! Look, you're country boys, you don't know the first thing

77

about working in the city. What can Télesphore do that's so special? Maybe he went to school a couple years more than we did, but that doesn't guarantee him a job in the city! He'll be greeted like all the others: like un habitant, one more habitant, come to live in the city and who smells like manure! That's what they say about us in the city, Josaphat, that we smell like manure! And what's more, they tell us in English! Because don't kid yourself, that's who you're going to work for! Because they've got the money! They say you smell like manure, you pretend you don't understand and you go right on serving them! Toute la gang! They tell you: "All right, all right!" as they give you a clap on the shoulder and they laugh at you behind your back! Our sister Ozéa's husband left ten years ago to deliver mail in an office of lawyers where they only speak English, thinking he'd become a lawyer some day, and what's he doing today? He delivers mail in his lawyers' office and he hasn't had a single raise in ten years. All he's learned in ten years is twenty-five words of English and they come out all wrong! That was his raise! But why are we talking about that, why are we still talking about that, Josaphat, I don't want to go to the city! I'd rather be an outcast looking at my own lake than a woman with no past living in a basement in the city! I think about Gabriel, God knows I think about Gabriel . . . I don't want to see him waste away in an alley, even if it's called la ruelle des Fortifications, and that's all.

LA GROSSE FEMME:
I often talk to him, Bartine . . . I have no problem . . .

ALBERTINE:
Ah, don't play your Madame Perfect with me, it drives me nuts!

VICTOIRE:
There's something else you have to think about,
Josaphat. Do you realize that my other children will be
by Télesphore?

She rushes into his arms.

VICTOIRE:
I can't prevent Télesphore from wanting children,
Josaphat! But I don't love him enough to give him any!
It's you I love, Josaphat!

LA GROSSE FEMME:
He even helps me to live. To go on living.

ALBERTINE:
Him? That tub of lard? Don't make me laugh!

LA GROSSE FEMME:
After your fights, when you slam the door and lock
yourself in your room, and you leave me alone with him . . .

ALBERTINE:
Ben oui, je le sais . . . I hear you talking, and laughing,
and I wonder what in God's name can they have to say
that's so much fun?

LA GROSSE FEMME:
You know what we always said about ton oncle
Josaphat . . . that he had a way of making us dream . . .

JOSAPHAT:
No one will keep me from giving you kids if I want
to, Victoire.

ALBERTINE:
Yeah, but he wasn't good for much else . . .

VICTOIRE:
Sure, every now and again we'll get together at a
family reunion and make a baby!

JOSAPHAT:
Ah, non, we'll have babies whenever we feel like it!

VICTOIRE: *(pulling away)*
Are you crazy? Are you crazy?

LA GROSSE FEMME:
Ben, Édouard is a bit like him, Bartine. It must be in
the family . . .

VICTOIRE:
If I marry Télesphore, Josaphat, it will be for good . . .

JOSAPHAT:
Do you really think I'd leave you alone? Do you think
I'm going to go stay in the city to watch you live from
a distance?

VICTOIRE:
Well, you can't come and live with us!

JOSAPHAT:
We can always work something out if we want to.

VICTOIRE:
And if I don't want to, hein? Télesphore is too good to
us, Josaphat, we can't spend our lives cheating on him!

LA GROSSE FEMME:
Sometimes, after we've had a good laugh, and we're
tired out, I sit in the rocker, especially in the summer
when the weather's nice and we can stay out late in
the evening . . . He sits beside me on his chair, or on

the floor . . . I put my hand on his arm or his shoulder, and I say to him . . . "Tell me everything, Édouard . . ." I close my eyes . . . I lay my head back and off I go . . . Far from la rue Fabre, far from the rest of you, far from myself . . . I walk down la rue St-Laurent, I climb the stairs of the French Casino . . . For sure it's another world, Bartine, for sure there're things we'll never know and we wouldn't want to know, either, but that's the point, it's something else! It's different from what we've always known, always will know . . .

ALBERTINE:
Ca, pour être différent . . .

LA GROSSE FEMME:
They have the most outlandish names, the people in his crowd, names they've invented or stolen from all sorts of places, books, the pictures . . . and they do the weirdest things . . . they all live in a dream, Bartine, it's as simple as that! They tell each other the wildest stories which they actually believe and when someone pricks their balloon, well, they just make up new ones. They sell shoes during the day or they work in offices, restaurants, banks, but at night they become someone else, someone famous, respected, rich . . . Mon Dieu, pourquoi pas . . . At times, the things Édouard tells me are so naïve, Bartine, a four-year-old wouldn't believe them, but he does! And it's beautiful that he does. And while he tells them to me, I believe them, too!

ALBERTINE:
You must have lots of time to kill!

LA GROSSE FEMME:
Ah, oui Bartine . . . Do I have time to kill! And you do, too! Édouard's stories help me to get through all

that time I have to kill! Don't you think it would do us good, you and me to dream we're someone else! If it weren't for him and his crazy dreams . . . they'd have locked me up a long time ago . . .

ALBERTINE:
You've got your books!

LA GROSSE FEMME:
Books cut you off from the world Bartine . . . We dream by ourselves when we read. And stories in books almost never happen here . . . With Édouard, it's like he really and truly lived all those things, you understand? And he shares them with me! He makes me dream right here, everything happens in my own city, sometimes with people I even know . . .

ALBERTINE:
But you said you don't believe them!

LA GROSSE FEMME:
I told you, I believe them at the time! Like when I read! But this way I'm not alone. I can answer his dreams, I can get inside them if I like . . . I can even change them because if I ask him to, he'll do it . . .

ALBERTINE:
I don't understand . . . I don't understand how a lot of nonsense from a fat brother-in-law who takes himself for . . . for a duchesse, can have that effect on you . . .

LA GROSSE FEMME:
Because you don't let yourself go . . .

ALBERTINE: *(aggressively)*
You bet I don't let myself go! Voyons donc! He's lying to our faces! You say so yourself!

LA GROSSE FEMME:
So use your imagination.

ALBERTINE:
I don't have any! And I don't want any! You see what it did to mon oncle Josaphat! And you see what it did to my little boy! My own child is a mixture of mon oncle Josaphat and my brother Édouard, you think that makes me want to join with them and say sure, go to it, be crazy, we'll have a good laugh? Everywhere I turn in my life, there are people like them! I don't understand what they are, I don't understand what they want! Day in and day out I live with a child I've never understood, isn't that enough? You think I'm gonna sit in a rocking chair and ask the other screwball to add his nonsense to that of my child, who I already don't understand? When my day is over, I have no wish to be somebody else! All I want to do is sleep! Sleep! And not to dream, but to forget! To forget, do you know what that means?

ÉDOUARD comes out of the house. He is dressed as at the beginning of the play.

ÉDOUARD:
This time they heard us in St-Jérôme! Talk a little louder, Bartine, and they'll hear you down in the States!

ALBERTINE:
Get dressed up a little more, Édouard, and they'll *see* you down in the States!

ÉDOUARD:
I'm not dressed up, now . . .

ALBERTINE:
Ouan, too bad . . . Our belle-soeur was just trying to convince me that you're more interesting dressed up . . .

LA GROSSE FEMME:
That's not what I said . . .

ÉDOUARD makes a sign, telling her not to answer.

LA GROSSE FEMME goes back to sit down on the steps.

JOSAPHAT:
When we were little, how we'd dream of Morial, you remember? We even dreamed of it with Télesphore . . .

VICTOIRE:
Ben oui, all three of us were children and we hated the country because in the summer we had to work on the farm and we'd dream of getting away. But that was twenty years ago . . .

ÉDOUARD:
When we were little, how we'd dream of Duhamel, you remember?

ALBERTINE:
We'd dream about it because we were bored in the city and we thought life was more interesting here . . .
And when we'd get here, we'd miss the city because it's boring here!

JOSAPHAT:
Now we're lucky, we can go there for good, like we wanted . . .

ÉDOUARD:
Now, we're lucky, we can spend a whole week out here . . .

VICTOIRE and ALBERTINE:
To hear you talk . . .

VICTOIRE:
. . . It's all decided, we're going to the city!

ALBERTINE:
. . . we've been dreaming about this for months!

VICTOIRE:
Just what are you going to do, in Morial, hein, apart
from being with me? Have you thought of that? You've
never worked in your life, Josaphat! All you know how
to do is make music! Do you really think you can earn
a living in the city with your fiddle?

ALBERTINE:
Just what are you going to do all week? Change your
costume twelve times a day? Go sing la chanson de la
Poune to the ducks at the end of the dock? Make up
more crazy stories to help our belle-soeur dream?

JOSAPHAT and ÉDOUARD:
You're always twisting things!

VICTOIRE and ALBERTINE:
Ben oui!

MATHIEU:
The truth of the matter is, you're a dreamer, Jean-
Marc. Like your grandfather. You always look so
composed, so centered, but you hardly ever weigh the
consequences of your actions.

JEAN-MARC:
This is the first time I've ever done something like
this. Let me try, Mathieu. For one year. Just let me

try. If it doesn't work . . . I'll step back in line, I
suppose . . . But if it does work . . . I have to prove
to myself that I can do more than churn out some little
courses for university, that I too can make the moon
come up . . . And the only place I can find out is here,
in this house. You understand?

They look at one another for a long moment.

MATHIEU:
Yeah, I suppose.

VICTOIRE:
I'm supposed to think everything is beautiful, is that it?
I can just see the two of us, happy as larks, down in
the basement on la ruelle des Fortifications . . . Sorry,
Josaphat, I can't . . .

ALBERTINE:
Sorry, Édouard, I can't . . . I can't listen to you as if
nothing was wrong . . . I know, this was all arranged in
advance, so just say what you've got to say, once and
for all! Forget the beautiful countryside and the lovely
week we're gonna spend! If it's up to me, Édouard,
our week, we'll spend it on le balcon de la rue Fabre,
because when you finish your big sermon, I'm packing
my bags!

ÉDOUARD:
Oh, boy, you sure know how to encourage conversation!
I can't say a word to you!

ALBERTINE:
Voyons donc! As if anyone could ever shut you up! Ah,
just say anything, what difference will it make?

ÉDOUARD:
> You mean after all that, you won't even listen? *(He turns towards his sister-in-law.)* I'm going to strangle her!

JOSAPHAT:
> They have dances in the city, Victoire! A lot more than here! Morial isn't some two-bit village where they hold a dance from time to time, it's a city full of people who want a good time after their week's work! So far, I've managed to earn us a living by going from town to town, one Saturday to the next, one dance to another, I'll do the same thing in the city, that's all! Folks will trample one another to get a good fiddler on a Saturday night. You watch, you'll admit I was right . . .

VICTOIRE:
> These are dreams . . .

JOSAPHAT:
> What do you mean, dreams? You said it yourself, a while ago, Morial is full of people who long for the country! Ben moé, I'll show them a good time! And my stories like la Chasse-Galerie, that you're always throwing back at me, I can adjust them for the city! I can make the moon rise in the city just as well as I can do it here!

VICTOIRE:
> Pretending to make the moon rise every night, Josaphat, never put food on anyone's table! You have the knack of never talking about the right things . . . Forget your stories, your stories won't cut any ice in the city! Folks there have seen a thing or two and they may not be interested in some guy who stomps his feet and tells crazy stories while he plays the fiddle! If nobody wants your stories in the city, what are you gonna do, hein? What are gonna do for the rest of your

87

life? Sweep the streets? Shovel snow? Stop dreaming,
Josaphat, for two minutes! If I marry Télesphore and
move to the city, it won't change a thing. What you're
really doing, Josaphat, is avoiding responsibility, as
usual! You're a child, a thirty-five year old child . . .
The minute something goes wrong, you turn your back
on it, you grab your maudit violon, and bingo, we have
a new jig! Because you know I'm there, right behind
you, and I'll try to patch things up . . . Here, I can
protect you, I do the best I can with what little money
you earn at your dances on Saturday night, but in the
city, Josaphat, you'll starve to death! Because you
can't defend yourself! Who's going to feed you,
Josaphat, me and Télesphore?

JOSAPHAT:
Victoire, how come you only see the bad side of things?

VICTOIRE:
Hé, que tu m'enrages! If I didn't have my two feet on
the ground, you and I would be six feet *under*ground,
ça fait longtemps!

He approaches her tenderly.

JOSAPHAT:
You don't really believe what you're saying . . .

VICTOIRE:
It's ture . . . Me too, deep down, I prefer your way
of seeing things . . . Malheureusement I'm more
realistic than you . . . My dreams don't last as long
and when they're over I don't have the imagination to
make up new ones . . . I have to wait for you . . . If
we're separated, Josaphat, what will I do? Will I spend
the rest of my life on the bad side of things?

He takes her in his arms.

JOSAPHAT:

Me, too, you know, I'm scared of the city. Too many people, too much électricité, too much noise . . . The unknown. No trees, no water, go for walks on wooden sidewalks, a little patch of sky . . . Mon Dieu. But most of all, I'm afraid there'll be no room . . . for la poésie.

VICTOIRE:

Then let's stay here, Josaphat . . . We've put up with everything for this long, we'll continue . . . We'll help each other . . .

JOSAPHAT:

We can't stay here, Victoire, not anymore . . . I had to sell the house to get myself started in the city . . .

She pulls away suddenly.

VICTOIRE:

To whom? Who did you sell the house to?

JOSAPHAT:

Don't worry . . . It'll stay in the family . . . I sold it to Ozéa's husband, who's looking for a maison de campagne . . .

VICTOIRE wails as if she had been struck.

ÉDOUARD:

It's true, I'd prepared a nice speech . . . and I'd worked up a whole production, too . . . I was going to take advantage of the fact that you were in the water or you were just coming out of the water . . . I was going to walk out on the dock . . . And I'd say to you . . . Non, ça, I must confess, I hadn't found the

89

beginning of our conversation . . . I was leaving that to
inspiration . . . I'd prepared everything else,
though . . . But now I can't use it. Because the
situation's not the same. You see, I wanted to take
advantage of the moment, to talk to you when neither
of us was dressed. That way, you couldn't accuse me
of being in disguise. But now . . . I don't feel natural in
my little suit and in the dark like this . . . In my mind,
it was beautiful, we were lying on our bath towels . . .
and you understood.

ALBERTINE: *(softly)*
Understood what, Édouard? Do you really think I don't
understand what you are? I don't accept it, but I
understand it. We didn't need a four hour ride in an
automobile to tell each other that . . . *(She moves
away from him.)* You've changed your clothes . . . but
your perfume . . . your woman's perfume is as strong
as ever.

ÉDOUARD:
I'm not wearing perfume, now . . .

ALBERTINE:
You always put on so much, Édouard, it never goes
away. We could find you in the middle of parc
Lafontaine, just by following your scent . . .

ÉDOUARD:
Tu vois, Bartine, what you just did now, that was
humour! If you hadn't said it seriously, if you'd had
said it with just a hint of a smile, we could have had a
good laugh, all three of us! It's not true you've no
imagination! Bartine, if you wanted to, you could be
so funny!

ALBERTINE: *(more aggressively)*
Sure, more laughter!

ÉDOUARD:
Ben oui, pourquoi pas? How do you think I made it
through everything that's happened to me? By
laughing, Bartine, especially when it wasn't funny!

ALBERTINE:
No one's interested in your tales of woe, Édouard . . .

ÉDOUARD:
I didn't come here to give you tales of woe, don't you
worry. *(Silence.)* Maudit, it's hard talking to you! No
wonder your kids are scared of you. You sure know
how to change the subject . . . I wanted to talk to you
about laughter, Bartine, laughter! When you get down
to it, whatever you accuse me of comes from the fact I
turn everything into a joke! If I didn't turn everything
into a joke, it's me who'd be the joke, Bartine. I laugh
before the others do. It's as simple as that! When I
walk down la rue Fabre dressed as la Poune, or
Madame Pétrie, and everyone laughs, I see them,
Bartine! Because I wanted them to laugh! I'd rather
they laugh in front of me, and with me, than behind my
back when I'm not there!

ALBERTINE:
You don't think they keep laughing after you've gone?
And they don't say what they really think once they're
back inside?

ÉDOUARD:
What difference does it make, if I got them started. If I
got them laughing on purpose? Remember last summer,
at la plage Roger, you were so ashamed of me because
I played the queen in front of a bunch of bums? Hein?

Well, if I hadn't played the queen in front of those bums, they'd have beaten the daylights out of me because they'd figured me out, right off the bat! If I'd tried to hide it, they'd have pestered me, they'd have pestered us, all day long, they'd have ruined our picnic and they'd have cornered me somewhere to insult me and beat me up! But I wiggled my ass for them, I stuck a napkin on my head and I sang them some old hits by Mistinguett, who they'd never heard of . . . and they laughed! All day long! They laughed all day long because I laughed at myself, all day long. At what I am, at my physique, the way I walk, the way I talk! I killed myself making them laugh, Bartine, to avoid having the day end badly. And by nightfall, they bought us all a round! By nightfall, they respected me! That's what I've discovered, Bartine, derision, to win the world's respect! Its respect!

ALBERTINE:
If you weren't the way you are, you wouldn't have to kill yourself to win respect . . .

ÉDOUARD:
Bartine, franchement! This is the way I am and that's all! There's nothing anyone can do, and above all, you mustn't try to change it!

ALBERTINE:
Stop trying to convince me it's not a serious matter! It is a serious matter, Édouard, and I can't accept it! I can't! When I think . . . When I think of what you do, I'd rather you were dead!

ÉDOUARD:
Then, don't think of what I do! In any case, you probably don't even know what I do . . .

ALBERTINE:
Sure, draw me a picture, while you're at it. It's not
just the dressing up and the foolery I can't accept,
Édouard! There's everything that's underneath, too!
Underneath your little suit that makes you uncomfortable,
there's a whole other man, my brother, who lives a life
that I reject! I know you continue to exist when you go
out the door. And underneath le personnage de la
semaine, there's another one, always the same, whom
I don't know, and who terrifies me! And you know
something, you're right, I do have an imagination,
because I often think about you during the week, at
night, about where you must be and what you might be
doing! And I'm so ashamed that if I didn't hold myself
back, I'd scream!

VICTOIRE begins to wail again.

JOSAPHAT:
Don't cry like that, Victoire . . .

VICTOIRE:
Notre maison . . . notre maison . . .

ÉDOUARD: *(to la Grosse Femme)*
Help me . . .

VICTOIRE:
And to get you started! But to get you started in what?
Making up tales of la Chasse-Galerie? In six months,
Josaphat, a year at the most, you'll have spent every
nickel, you have no idea what money is! You've no idea
what things cost, it's always me who pays! To get
yourself started! But it won't be the beginning of
something, it will be the end of everything!

JOSAPHAT can't answer.

ALBERTINE:
Don't force yourselves, either one of you . . .

JOSAPHAT:
You won't lose everything . . . I was going to give you half the money . . .

VICTOIRE:
But I don't want it! It's not money I want, it's ma maison! I know, papa left it to you but you didn't have the right to sell it without asking me . . .

JOSAPHAT:
You would have stopped me . . .

VICTOIRE:
Ben certain! Certain! I'd have done anything to keep you from selling it! And, tonight, you had the nerve to tell Gabriel about la maison suspendue!

JOSAPHAT:
I want him to have the most wonderful memories . . . and you, you said if you left, you'd never come back . . . so what does it matter if the house has been sold . . .

VICTOIRE: *(as if exhausted)*
I said that because I didn't really think we'd be leaving . . . Now, I believe it . . . For the first time, I believe it . . . Now, I know I'm going to marry Télesphore, that we'll move to the city, that Gabriel will grow up in the noise and the dirt . . . but I also know that never again, never, will I let you come near me. *(She closes her eyes.)* Even though I love you. Don't bother coming to Morial to see me, Josaphat, you won't see me. Go live somewhere else.

She moves away from JOSAPHAT. She puts her hands on her belly.

VICTOIRE:

Looks like you'll be born in the city . . . If you're a boy, I'll call you Josaphat, so I'll have the right to say that name as often as possible for the rest of my days . . . If you're a girl, I'll call you Albertine, like my mother's mother, in the hopes you'll be as kind and gentle as her . . . Non, if you're a girl you won't be kind, I know it. You are going to . . . you're going to inherit the very worst in me, you'll inherit all my rage for being forced to leave the country and to go bury myself in the city . . . You won't know it, but you will carry with you . . . all my sorrows . . . I won't be able to keep from passing my sorrows on to you . . . and to your children. *(Silence.)* This may be the last time I speak to you.

She disappears into the darkness, in the direction of the suspended well.

JOSAPHAT:

The cord is cut. The house will stay here. The canoe is drifting away . . . When we tie up in Morial, Gabriel is the only one who'll disembark. Victoire and I will stay in the canoe forever . . . Two lost souls in a birch bark canoe, washed up on a crowded shore. Everything I've done is so my son won't be an outcast, so he won't have to pay for his parents' beautiful sin. I've assumed my responsibilities as a father, as head of the family . . . I've sacrificied everything so my son will never be pointed at again. I'm not irresponsible. Even if I know that Morial has no use for my fiddle!

ALBERTINE:

It's true, it was a nice image . . . the two of us at the

end of the dock, with our belle-soeur on her chaise longue . . . No noise . . . Just the water lapping on the dock . . . it smells a bit of muck . . . *(She closes her eyes.)* I wish I knew how . . .

ÉDOUARD approaches her.

ÉDOUARD:

It's still possible . . . It's up to you. The sun is hot . . . you have your towel on your shoulders because it's the first time you've been out in ages . . . You suspect I want to talk to you . . . Moé, I climb out of the water like a big whale, dripping all over the place . . . I get down on all fours on the dock, and I wiggle my bum, spraying you with water, just like when we were little . . . then, I lie on my back, my paws in the air, my tongue hanging out . . . you laugh. You laugh, Bartine! And because you laugh, I decide now is the time.

He takes her by the shoulders rather like the beginning an operatic duo.

ÉDOUARD:

Bartine . . . Bartine . . .

ALBERTINE:

Quoi, donc . . .

ÉDOUARD:

Things aren't going well for me these days . . . What I earn selling shoes isn't enough since Samarcette left . . . I spoke to Gabriel about it, and our belle-soeur . . . For a while, I'd like to take back my room in the house. Not for good . . . just for a while. Take my place again. Because I'm having a hard time. Because I'm lonely. And I need the rest of you.

He kisses her passionately on the neck.

She rests her head on his shoulder.

ALBERTINE: *(exhausted, a bit like her mother, earlier)*
Let's say the scene is finished. Let's say the dream is
finished. You've told me everything.

ÉDOUARD:
And what did you answer . . .

*She turns around suddenly, clinging to him and
weeping.*

LA GROSSE FEMME turns away.

ÉDOUARD:
If you say yes, you know-you'll have to put up with la
Poune, and madame Pétrie, and Shirley Temple, and
the whole shebang.

She stiffens.

VICTOIRE reappears on the opposite side of the stage.

*JEAN-MARC gets up slowly and comes to sit next to
his mother.*

JEAN-MARC:
I've always thought of myself as the nobody in the
family. The least complicated. The least interesting. I
was born a long time after Marcel, I was the last one
in the three families . . . I was fairly quiet. I watched
all the others struggle with their bad times, their good
times too because they couldn't deal with happiness
either . . . It all seemed so ridiculous to me. That life

97

made no sense if everything was so complicated. I
didn't want my life to be complicated like theirs . . .
And one day, out here, in August . . . We'd come
here to spend a few days, my mother and father, my
two brothers and me . . . I was younger than Sébastien
at the time . . . The week went by with no big
problems, although it was a bit strange to find
ourselves like that, just the five of us . . . I think it
was the first time. We were always caught up in the
great family saga of la rue Fabre. Any real family life
was impossible and my mother, especially, suffered
from that . . . Anyway, around the middle of the
week, my mother said to us: "Don't follow
me . . . I'm going to the lake, but don't anybody follow
me . . . " She had put on an old house dress she
never wore anymore and that was torn under the
arms . . . A bit worried, I watched her go . . . My
mother never asked us not to follow her. My father
and my brothers had to go into Duhamel anyway,so off
they went. I stayed here. I sat down, exactly where I
am now. And I looked off in the direction of the lake.
You can't see the water's edge from here, because of
the steep decline; all you can see is the end of the
dock jutting out into the water . . . My mother wasn't
on the dock. What in the world could she be doing in
her house dress on the shore of the lake? Then all of a
sudden, maybe after half an hour, I heard this little cry.
Not a cry of fear, or of surprise, just a little cry. I ran
toward the lake. Next to the dock, there is a stone
stairway that goes into the water, you'll see it
tomorrow, Mathieu. It must have been for tying up
boats, or something, I don't know . . . My
mother . . . my mother who had trouble getting into
the bathtub in the city, because of her size, and who
always said she had to wash herself one parish at a
time . . . my mother had stepped down into the water
in her house dress . . . She was sitting on the bottom

step of the stairway, so she was in the water about up
to her shoulders . . . She splashed around a
bit . . . and she let out these little cries of joy that she
couldn't contain . . . I was quite close, hidden behind a
birch tree, and I could see her in profile . . . I had
never seen a face like that . . . She had raised her
face towards the sun, I could see her hands splashing
the water about . . . Her house dress ballooned out
around her, and she'd give it little whacks to get the
air out . . . I didn't know that woman, Mathieu. How
long had it been since she had gone into the water like
that? And all of a sudden, she threw her head back and
she started to laugh . . . The laugh of a happy child
who discovers the water of a lake the first time . . .
The countryside lifted right up, I saw my mother, the
dock, the lake, the mountains lift right up into the sky,
like they do in mon oncle Josaphat's stories, and I said
to myself: "Life isn't complicated. Life does make
sense. Life makes sense, my mother's laughing!"

LA GROSSE FEMME bursts out laughing.

JEAN-MARC:
How often I find I miss that laugh. When life gets
complicated. Like it is now. She's been gone for
twenty-seven years and I still miss her.

LA GROSSE FEMME:
When we get up tomorrow, we'll all go for a swim!

The door of the house swings open, the boy comes out.

MATHIEU:
Sébastien, tu dors pas?

ALBERTINE:
What are you doing up at this hour?

VICTOIRE:

Gabriel, you'll catch cold . . .

THE CHILD:

I heard voices . . . *(He places himself between Jean-Marc and la Grosse Femme.)* It's too hot in my room . . . Can I stay with you for a bit?

VICTOIRE:

Go put your stockings on . . .

THE CHILD:

I already have!

MATHIEU bends down on his knees behind his son and puts his arms around his shoulder.

MATHIEU:

A lot has happened in this house, Sébastien . . . A long time ago . . . Things . . . things that had nothing to do with us because they happened to people we didn't know . . . but they're things that concern us, now. Things we'll have to learn . . . to add . . . to our lives. This house belongs to us, to Jean-Marc, to papa, and to you, too, a little bit . . . but you and I will have to learn to deserve it . . .

VICTOIRE turns towards the lake.

VICTOIRE:

Adieu, mon lac! On s'en va. We're abandoning you. Try not to miss us as much as we'll miss you. Keep us in you, keep our imprints, keep the imprint of our bodies around the dock and I will keep your imprint . . . in my heart. Keep our smells . . . our laughter . . . our swims across, as if we'd wanted to cut you in half. Keep the tracks of our snowshoes in winter, when we tramped over you on our way to Duhamel. *(Silence.)* We'll never see each other again. Never. Take a good look at me. It's the last time you'll see me. I'm leaving. For the city. *(Silence.)* Josaphat! Josaphat! Call up the devil! It's time to go!

We hear a very energetic jig.

La maison suspendue, hanging from the end of a rope, hooked onto a birchbark canoe by a ship's anchor, flies over the sky of Duhamel. The canoe is guided by the Devil himself, who points the way towards the city.

As they huddle, one against the other, all the characters watch the house sail away.

BLACK

X